LEARNING EXAM SKILLS

D0582558

LEARNING
EXAM
SKILLS

Harry McVea, LLB, PhD
Lecturer in Law, University of Bristol

Peter Cumper, LLB
Senior Lecturer in Law,
Nottingham Trent University

BLACKSTONE PRESS LIMITED

First published in Great Britain 1996 by Blackstone Press Limited,
Aldine Place, London W12 8AA. Telephone 0181-740 2277

© Harry McVea and Peter Cumper 1996

ISBN: 1 85431 451 3

Reprinted 1999

British Library Cataloguing in Publication Data
A CIP catalogue record for this book is available from the British Library

Typeset by Style Photosetting Limited, Mayfield, East Sussex
Printed by Livesey Limited, Shrewsbury, Shropshire

All rights reserved. No part of this book may be reproduced or transmitted in
any form or by any means, electronic or mechanical, including photocopying,
recording, or any information storage or retrieval system without prior
permission from the publisher.

Contents

Contents

Preface

This book is intended for students taking academic law exams. Unlike some other books which cater for a similar readership, we do not aim merely to provide a series of model answers to questions posed. Although some students may find such books helpful, we believe that pedagogically they are of limited value and are apt, in many instances, to leave a student floundering when a new question is raised or an issue which has already been addressed is presented in a slightly modified form. Neither do we cover the more mundane issues relating to examinations such as revision, division of time between questions, and so on, since these are problems which students who are taking law exams will already have encountered and mastered in their earlier studies. However, because certain aspects of law examinations are different from other exams which most students will have taken, the aim here is to focus on the *process* of taking exams. In particular, we aim to demonstrate how good students can do justice to themselves by adopting the *techniques* employed by successful examinees. Suggestions are made as to ways in which materials can be manipulated and legal arguments marshalled; and methods are identified by which both essay and, more especially, problem questions can be approached. For reasons of space, we have chosen to limit our analysis to the core subjects of criminal law, torts, contract, and public law. However, the techniques employed are broadly applicable to other law courses such as land law, trusts, evidence, and so on. Likewise, although we concentrate on unseen timed exams, our suggestions are also relevant to open book exams, take-home exams and course work assessment. The chapters in the problem questions part of the book are not self-standing. Instead, the general approach we adopt is set out in chapter 1 and is subsequently reinforced and – where appropriate – modified in the remaining chapters. Authorial comment is in square brackets and in a bold font. Edited parts of the answers are indicated by asterisks.

   Though the origins of *Learning Exam Skills* go back to when we ourselves were law students, more recently we have been faced with a different version of the same problem as law teachers. Often good students fail to reach their full potential on paper, not because they have neglected or are unable to understand the relevant rules and principles of the law, but because of a failure to master exam technique. The need to *teach* students how to answer law questions and to explain to them why one answer is better than another has prompted us to think about this problem in a more systematic way and, ultimately, to crystallise our thoughts by writing this book. While it is by no means the definitive guide on exam technique, we hope that it will help students produce work which better reflects their true abilities and, perhaps, make our task of reading and marking exam answers more pleasant.

In undertaking this endeavour we owe a great debt of gratitude to colleagues, friends, and former teachers without whose help – and ideas – this project would not have been possible. In particular, we would like to thank Dr Michael Knight who, as our criminal law tutor at the Queen's University of Belfast, presented us with our first systematic insights into answering law examination questions. We would also like to thank Paul Robinson for providing assistance with the references and, last, but by no means least, we extend our thanks to our publishers who remained patient and helpful throughout.

Harry McVea, University of Bristol
Peter Cumper, Nottingham Trent University

Introduction

How do you succeed in law school? This deceptively simple, perennial question is asked by every generation of law students. On the face of it there would appear to be no easy answer. After all, those who are awarded the highest marks are not always those with the most information. Admittedly, a good memory, staying calm under exam conditions, allocating time, and writing quickly and clearly all have a part to play. Yet the single most important factor in most instances is, in our view, *exam technique*. While for some students exam technique may be intuitive – they don't have to think about it because they just have it – the point is that exam technique *can* be acquired. It can be learned, provided students are prepared to let go of their old habits and take on board new ways of handling the material they have been set to master. Moreover, if students were required, as part of their learning experience, to mark answers – and see their own work as examiners see it – they would undoubtedly perform more successfully in their exams. The changes required in terms of *content* and *style* to earn the really high marks would become readily apparent.

From the outset students should be aware that the thesis underpinning this book – that such a thing as exam technique exists and that it can (and should) be acquired – is controversial. There are three basic views on this question:

(a) *Exam technique cannot be taught.* First, there are those who believe that what we have proposed cannot be done. Adherents to this school argue either (i) that answering legal exam questions is a skill – something which you either have or you don't have – a skill which it is impossible to articulate and therefore to teach; or (ii) that there is no one method – that each tutor expects something different, with the result that the 'right' exam technique depends on the preferences of each individual examiner.

(b) *Exam technique should not be taught.* Secondly, there are those who believe that university education operates best by encouraging people to think for themselves by fending for themselves. To do otherwise is 'anti-intellectual';

it would drag good students down and pull mediocre students up, thus frustrating one of the basic aims of university education – to let the talented flourish. Good students, so this argument runs, will get to grips with the necessary techniques without specific instruction.

(c) *Exam technique should be taught.* Lastly there are those – like us – who believe that exam technique can, and should, be taught; that it is part of the process of teaching students 'how to think'. While there is certainly something to be said for the idea that answering exam questions is a skill, skills often need to be nurtured and developed; and although different academics do appear to have their own preferences in relation to answering exam questions, there is a great deal of agreement as to what is quality work and how legal questions should be framed and answered. The argument that exam technique should not be taught smacks of 'hiding the ball' from students, and taken to its logical conclusion could apply to all forms of teaching.

The strongest argument against those who advocate that exam technique is capable of being, and should be, taught is that it is tinged with an unwarranted degree of dogmatism – by implying that a certain way is the 'right' way of handling the relevant materials. This appears to put students in intellectual strait-jackets, lending credence to the view that teaching exam technique is 'unacademic'. If this were true, such criticism would be valid. However, this argument misrepresents the context of the case for teaching exam skills as we present it: that there are a number of ways of demonstrating good exam technique, in amongst which the approach we emphasise is merely one. In any case, exceptional students are unlikely to be hampered by our prescriptive approach, but will rise above it. Competent students, on the other hand, are likely to benefit. And while we recognise that individuality and creativity should be encouraged amongst *all* students, the reality of the situation is that students have to sit exams. Although these should by no means be viewed as the sole aim of the educational process, it would be disingenuous to ignore exams completely.

The problem is that to teach what is in effect a subtle skill, one must simplify and illustrate by way of 'crude' examples, just to get the point across. Again, let us stress that we have not set out to write a definitive work on answering examination questions. Neither should students assume that the techniques set out are to be slavishly followed or applied in a purely mechanical fashion. They will need to be 'fine-tuned' and it may on occasion be necessary to adapt our suggestions – jettisoning some points and adding others – to accommodate a student's own insights into a subject or, more pragmatically, to accord with individual tutors' preferences. Indeed, if anything your tutor says conflicts with what we have suggested, follow your tutor's advice – for that course at least. The aim, after all, is to increase the chances of exam success rather than to reduce them.

EXAM OBJECTIVES

Before we proceed to discuss these techniques it is first necessary to consider what law exams are designed to test i.e., their objectives. No doubt there are many objectives, but for present purposes we can say that exams are designed to test a student's ability to:

1. Identify legal issues.
2. Display knowledge of legal rules and principles.
3. Apply the law to complex fact situations.
4. Distinguish between the relevant and the irrelevant.
5. Analyse and evaluate legal doctrines.
6. Construct coherent, logical and persuasive arguments.
7. Work under pressure, subject to time constraints.

As a rule examiners do not explicitly refer to these objectives; neither do they have a definitive list of points which must be covered, still less a 'model' of what the answer should look like. Yet despite the scope that this gives for an impressionistic and subjective approach to exam marking, there exists a remarkable degree of unanimity amongst examiners when it comes to spotting good answers. Although it is difficult to say exactly why this is so, it may not be too much of an exaggeration to suggest that an examiner is as interested in the *method* or *approach* by which the question has been addressed as he or she is in whether the student has given the 'right answer', insofar as a right answer exists. One final point should be noted in this section. Although there should be a direct link between the way in which a course is taught and the way in which it is assessed, sadly this is not always the case. For example, sometimes the lecturer(s) will pay only lip-service to the theoretical aspects of a subject, yet the exam will require a detailed knowledge of theory. Be sensitive to this problem by looking at past exam papers to see how well the examination reflects the material covered in the course.

What examiners are looking for in determining whether students achieve the above objectives can be expressed at different levels of abstraction, many of which are decidedly unhelpful. At the highest level, they are looking for an answer which is written in a 'lawyerly fashion'. At a more concrete level this means that you must handle the material not only *competently*, but also *confidently*, and it is the combination of these two components which will mark you out as a first class candidate. More specifically, your answer must be characterised by a thorough, balanced, logical analysis of the legal issues, supported by authority (case law, statutory, academic) and written in a clear and concise fashion. It is, however, fair to say that most law students know this already. They are probably used to hearing about the necessity of cultivating the skill of systematic legal analysis – the hallmark of an accomplished lawyer. But for many, either it does not sink in, or they do not know what it means or entails when it comes to answering exam questions. They are unsure of what questions to ask to help them structure their answers; they do not know how to identify the relevant legal issues, analyse them, or introduce and manipulate supporting authority. There is, of course, nothing particularly mysterious about these tasks. All one has to do is to open a law report or a law journal. In the former you will see how judges address legal issues, present arguments and cite relevant authorities; in the official law reports, such as the appeal cases, just before the start of the judgments, you can see how this is done by counsel for each party. In law journals the process is repeated, either in the longer articles or in the much shorter casenotes and comments. Ultimately, these are the models you should emulate in terms of style and technique and it is from these sources that we draw many of our ideas and some of our examples. But to leave it at that is not sufficient. Despite the fact that what judges, barristers, and academics do – address legal problems, present arguments, manipulate authorities, and so on – is similar to what you must do, your task still differs in significant respects. Your questions come pre-packaged, in 'crime boxes', or 'contract boxes', etc. Generally when you answer an unseen question, your answer is based on what you can recall, and as you are often subject to time constraints, what you write must be both relevant and concise. The most important difference, however, is that in the law reports judges normally focus on specific ingredients (sub-issues) of the particular crime, tort, or whatever is being discussed, rather than on the general ingredients of the offence, tort etc. The reason for this is that most of the cases you are asked to read are at the appellate stage and therefore the legal questions have already been pared down to their fundamentals. By contrast, in the exam you must demonstrate that you understand *all* the basic elements of the legal issue concerned (a crime, tort, breach of contract, and so on), even though you are entitled to focus on the ones which are particularly relevant to the question set. The basic rule of thumb is that you cannot rely on examiners to infer that you know these things. You should assume that they know very little (general knowledge excepted) about the subject and that it is up to you to provide an appropriate explanation of the relevant issues. The rest of this book is aimed at advising students how this can be done to good effect.

TYPES OF EXAM QUESTIONS

The starting point for our discussion of exam technique concerns the nature of the questions with which law students are faced. Basically, these are of two types: problem questions and essay questions. Although in some respects a good essay will display all of the hallmarks of a good problem answer (in that it will contain a logical and well-written analysis of the legal issues posed, supported by authority), the approach required for each is essentially different. The student who fails to grasp this important point at the outset of his or her studies will fail to do justice to himself or herself in the end of year examinations.

Because of the different techniques required to answer both essay and problem questions, the book is divided into two (unequal) parts: Part A dealing with problem questions and Part B dealing with essay questions. The reason for this imbalance is that many students studying law for the first time will have been previously fed on an 'exam diet' of essays, and thus answering problem questions will be unfamiliar territory to them. It is not surprising therefore that a significant number of students display a natural aversion to problem solving, or have difficulty getting to grips with it. Whether this arises as a result of greater familiarity with essay writing, or because of a pragmatic belief that essays offer more of an opportunity to introduce into their answers material which they have learned but which is not directly relevant to the question posed (unlike problems, which require a more definite 'answer') is unclear. But regardless of reasons, it is simply not possible to excel in your law exams (or in legal practice) unless you acquire the art of problem-solving. Indeed, with the correct approach, it is easier to score very high marks in a problem question than it is in an essay.

Despite the fact that all problem questions deal with the same basic legal issue – what are the rights and liabilities of the parties? – in each subject this takes a different form. We have chosen to draw our examples from criminal law, contract, torts, and public law. For example, in criminal law the central issues are the crimes which the defendant has committed and what, if any, defences are available. In torts the format is similar, but here we are interested in the defendant's wrongs and what, if any, the applicable defences are. In contract the issue is who can sue, be sued, on what grounds, and with what consequences? In public law, meanwhile, you may simply be asked to comment on the constitutional propriety of the events in a problem and a range of sanctions (criminal, civil, or even political) may be relevant to your answer. Thus, although all legal problem questions are in essence the same – and many of the techniques explored in one section are capable of being duplicated in another – there are nonetheless good reasons why in Part A, each of the chosen subjects should be dealt with separately. In particular, it makes possible the identification and explanation of our basic ideas in chapter 1 (on criminal law), and the reinforcement and modification (where necessary) of those ideas in chapters 2 (torts), 3 (contract), and 4 (public law). The division of chapters also makes possible the identification and application of what might be called 'micro' structures relating to specific topics in each subject which will help you in answering exam questions in these areas. The most obvious example of such a micro structure in torts would be the 'duty, breach, damage' formula used in answering negligence questions. For an exemption clause question, it would be 'incorporation' (is the exclusion clause a term in the contract?), 'construction' (does the clause cover the breach?), and 'legislative factors' (e.g., what is the effect of EC and UK legislation on unfair contract terms?).

In contrast to the organising framework adopted for problem questions, we propose to deal with essay questions collectively, since we are of the opinion that the techniques for answering essay questions are unlikely to vary at all according to subject-matter.

PART A

PROBLEM QUESTIONS

Chapter 1

Criminal Law

It is important to note that many of the suggestions in this chapter will be of use in answering questions in other areas of law, and are not applicable only to those areas discussed in this book. The relevant patterns will become clear as we tackle the subjects covered. Another important point to stress is that each chapter assumes a detailed knowledge of the relevant law – in this instance, a detailed knowledge of the applicable crimes, their ingredients (i.e., the *actus reus* and *mens rea*) and any supporting authority. In addition, it is assumed that the reader is fully acquainted with the appropriate defences and the rules by which they may be invoked, again supported by authority. While there is no substitute for this kind of detailed knowledge, it is also crucial that it is properly compartmentalised, otherwise you will have no means by which to access it, and thus no way of processing it in the way required of a good student. Knowledge (properly compartmentalised) and technique fit together like hand and glove.

1. IDENTIFYING THE LEGAL ISSUES

Problem questions are complex stories, within which are hidden a number of legal issues which you must identify and proceed to discuss. This discussion should involve an outline of the relevant legal principles and an application of them to the key facts in such a way as to reach a credible conclusion. Your first and most important task is then to formulate the problem, not by reference to its facts, but in terms of the legal issues raised by the facts. As mentioned earlier, in criminal law problems the issue will always deal with the crime(s) with which the defendant can be charged – murder, manslaughter, s. 18, Offences Against the Persons Act 1861 (OAPA) and so on – and the defences available on the charges alleged.

Of course, at first glance the problem may seem really obvious and you may feel that you have identified all of the legal issues – which indeed you may, depending on how immersed you are in your course or how naturally talented you are at issue-spotting. Alternatively the problem may seem completely impenetrable, in that you may feel unable to identify any or all of the relevant legal issues. However, the issues are there. In fact, in devising the exam question the examiner has started with the legal issues he or she wishes to test and has woven a story around them. For example, the examiner might decide to test s. 18, OAPA 1861/ duress/ participation:

Alan, a journalist, with the Bloomsbury Bee, has written an article critical of Cedric, a well-known terrorist leader. Alan's colleague, David, accepts an invitation to play golf at Cedric's country club. After 18 holes, Cedric informs David that if he does not bring to him, by the end of the day, the index finger from Alan's right hand, he will kill David's wife and three-year-old son. David reluctantly agrees and takes the knife which Cedric has given him. Later that day David drives to Alan's home and severely injures him.

Consider the criminal liability of David and Cedric.

How, then, do you make sure that you have identified the legal issues which the examiner has set? Well, one method, which if nothing else will keep you on the right track, is to make a mental list of all the crimes covered on your criminal law course. This list would contain the relevant offences against the person (from murder down to assault). It would also have all of the main property offences: theft, burglary (different types), deception (different types), robbery, making off without payment etc. You might draw a circle round both groups of offences to illustrate attempts (and other inchoate offences) and participation. Your list would also contain all the defences, noting any peculiarities (e.g., that provocation is only a defence to murder). This list would then act as your template, with which to identify the legal issues posed by the problem question. Thus if someone has died you would know that your answer would involve a discussion of either murder or manslaughter (and if the latter a specification of the relevant type(s)). Alternatively, if the harm suffered was minor, you should look to technical assault or battery; if it was serious, s. 18, OAPA 1861 or s. 20, OAPA 1861, and so on. Once you have classified the harm you can then focus on the defendant's *mens rea* to pin-point the most appropriate charge. It is absolutely crucial at this stage that you read the question carefully and that you get the facts, the parties, and what was done by whom, sorted out. If you do not your answer will be off target.

Consider the above example involving Alan, David, and Cedric. In attempting to isolate the issues, clearly you need a working knowledge of the various crimes covered on your course – which you should be able to glean either from memory or from the template suggested earlier. Of course, in reality there are many more offences, some of which would be relevant to the facts, but for the purposes of the exam you do not need to know these – for that, knowledge of the crimes covered on the syllabus is sufficient. Since you are told that Alan is severely injured (and by implication not dead) you should be thinking in terms of either a s. 20, OAPA 1861, or, most probably, a s. 18, OAPA charge against David – because these are generally the only offences you will cover which involve serious injury (GBH) short of death. Although David intentionally, albeit reluctantly, causes Alan to sustain GBH, it is clear that David is acting under compulsion, so the defence of duress should spring to mind – but, if not, check your list of possible alternative defences. Even a basic understanding of these will tell you that duress is the only option. You should also consider Cedric's liability. After all, he did supply David with the knife which severely injured Alan. As a result, the issue arises as to whether Cedric is liable for aiding and abetting the main/principal offence.

That, then, is your *thinking process*. But what should you write? The first paragraph of your answer could set out the relevant crimes with which the defendant will be charged and any defences he might have available to him. Weaker students tend not to do this either because they do not know exactly what the issues are, or because they are afraid of committing themselves to issues that are not actually there or which are totally irrelevant. Your first paragraph might be something along the following lines:

> The main issue in this problem is whether David has available to him the defence of duress on a s. 18, OAPA 1861 charge (intent to do GBH). The problem also raises the issue of Cedric's liability arising out of his participation in the principal offence and his threats to David.

Here the answer clearly *implies* that David is likely to face a s. 18 charge and that in relation to that charge he may wish to use the defence of duress. The issue of Cedric's liability in the scheme is raised, although the exact nature of the charges is left to be addressed later in the answer.

An alternative – and probably better – approach would be as follows:

> The first issue is whether the defendant is guilty of a s. 18, OAPA 1861 offence (intending GBH) and, if he is, whether he will be able to rely on the defence of duress. . . . **[You could then go on to discuss these points.]**

> * * *

> The second issue is whether C is liable as an aider and abettor on a s. 18 OAPA 1861 charge. . . . **[You could then go on to discuss this.]**

> * * *

> The third issue is . . .

The advantage of this approach is that you do not commit yourself too early to the issues raised and you are able to add new charges as and when you think of them, while progressing through your answer.

Since first impressions matter, your opening paragraph is likely to be important. Therefore, you must demonstrate right from the outset that you are in control of the material. In fact very often the examiner will, within the first ten lines or so, build up a presumption – whether consciously or subconsciously – of the class of mark he or she will award to your script. While what is written thereafter may rebut or confirm that presumption, your introduction sets the tone.

Sometimes students start by writing:

In discussing the criminal liability of David and Cedric it is necessary to establish what offences they can be charged with.

But what does something like this add? Surely it is axiomatic that in a criminal law exam, you need to do this. Other students like to write a general introduction to a problem question covering the area of law they have been asked to address. Somehow it helps them 'feel' their way into the question. For example, in answering the above problem a student might write:

This question deals mainly with the law on duress which has recently been the subject of much judicial concern, the main issue being whether duress should be a defence to murder. In the widely criticised decision in *Howe*, the House of Lords ruled that duress was not available on a murder charge. Their Lordships were of the opinion that the harshness of the ruling could be tempered by Executive discretion on whether or not to prosecute.

Here David will be charged with . . .

Although opinions do vary, introductions of the above type are best avoided when answering a problem question. While generally you will not lose marks by adopting the above approach, you are unlikely to gain many either. Why? It is not that what has been written is incorrect, but rather that the student's knowledge has been misdirected. This sort of introduction fails to focus on the questions posed: the criminal liability of David and Cedric. Instead, it goes off at a tangent, discussing issues which are not germane to the question. This serves as a reminder that doing well in exams is as much about knowing what to leave out (because it is not strictly relevant) as it is about knowing what to include. As we suggested earlier, one of the purposes of exams is to see whether students can distinguish the relevant from the irrelevant. In answering a problem question you should address yourself directly to the question asked and answer it as concisely as possible.

Sometimes students begin answers by summarising the facts of the problem. This too should be avoided. The examiner knows the facts: he or she will have set the problem, and if not, will have a copy of it to hand. The facts should be used sparingly, and only in relation to the application of legal principles to them, or when you are attempting to distinguish your fact pattern from a case which prima facie applies to it.

Another commonly used student approach is to begin an answer by saying that the facts of the problem bear a resemblance to the facts of a particular case studied (for more on this type of approach to answering questions generally, see pp. 35–36). For example, if the question is:

> D, a tramp, suffers from schizophrenia. To keep himself warm he lights a fire in a haystack. The fire gets out of control and the haystack is destroyed. Discuss.

A typical student answer might read something like this:

> The facts in the problem are similar to the facts of *R* v *Stephenson*, where it was held that 'recklessness' meant subjective recklessness, i.e., foreseeing the risk but carrying on regardless . . .

But by starting off with a case, the student has cited an authority which is no longer good law. The meaning of 'recklessness', in the context of criminal damage, now has an objective meaning (see *Caldwell* [1982] AC 341). (As an aside, you may have wondered why law lecturers tell you about cases that are no longer good law. Students must grasp early on in their studies the difference between (i) what the law is, (ii) areas where it is (or is thought to be) unclear, (iii) what the different options are for clarification or law reform, and (iv) what commentators think the law ought to be. Your lecturer could have talked about *Stephenson* [1979] 1 QB 695, for example, to illustrate aspects of (iii) and (iv). In addition, some areas of law are better (or can only be) understood in terms of their historical development.)

Even if a student starts off with a case that is good law, problems remain:

Question

> D and his friends, A and B, have just finished their last drinks of the evening, whereupon D invites A and B to go to his house so that they can have sexual intercourse with his wife, V. D tells them that they should not be at all alarmed if V struggles and protests, because this is how she gets her 'kicks'. Before, during, and after intercourse V is an unwilling participant. Discuss.

A typical student answer might read something like this:

Answer

> The facts in the problem are similar to the facts of *DPP* v *Morgan*, where the House of Lords dismissed the defendant's appeals, on the basis that although the trial judge had misdirected the jury, a properly directed jury would have reached the same verdict anyway. In *Morgan* the husband had been charged with aiding and abetting rape, while the others were charged with rape. The court had to determine whether . . .

Again, although there is nothing incorrect in the above answer, this type of introduction is best avoided. By telling the examiner that the facts are similar to *Morgan*, your answer gets off on the wrong foot. Your material is probably better presented in terms of the legal issues raised by the question rather than in terms of similar facts. If you must start off with the case, try:

In *DPP* v *Morgan* (a case on similar facts) the House of Lords held that where, on a rape charge, defendant honestly and genuinely, albeit unreasonably, believed that the women consented to the sexual intercourse, he is to have available to him the 'defence' of mistaken belief **[but now you are faced with the problem of having put the defence before having stated the offence]**.

To recap, there is no need to write a traditional essay-type introduction, neither is there any need to launch into a long-winded regurgitation of the facts of the problem or to start off comparing it to cases with similar facts. Instead your answer needs to cut to the heart of the problem. As we shall see in the next section, it needs to be pithy and supported by authority at every opportunity. Hard earned knowledge should not get in the way of addressing the issues directly.

2. STRUCTURING YOUR ANSWER

In view of time constraints and other exam pressures it is not surprising that most students fail to structure their answers. But although such a failure is understandable, it does not excuse the 'stream of consciousness' approach which many students adopt in exams, where their answers lurch from one point to the next with no particular aim in mind except that of unloading on to the answer booklet as much as possible of what they have learned. Structure is, however, absolutely crucial, and it is false economy – except in a genuine emergency – to launch straight into your answer without taking some time to think about how you will present your material. To put it another way: in students' terms, a lecture which is crammed full of information is useless unless it is presented within a good, clear, tight framework; in examiners' terms, a student answer needs to be similarly presented, indicating clearly the development of the material constituting the answer. An examiner wants to read a clear, well thought out script in the same way that a students wants to listen to a clear, well thought out lecture. More students would do well to remember that (i) a little information can go a long way if it is presented in a clear, concise and digestible fashion; and (ii) students who are awarded the highest marks in the exam are not necessarily those with the most information.

Consider the following problem:

Bernie is mentally subnormal. He drives his car to a petrol station and fills it with petrol. He is over-charged by the cashier. Losing his temper, he picks up the cashier's full cup of tea and throws it in his face. The cup accidentally slips from Bernie's hand and cuts the cashier's face.

Bernie storms outside and absent-mindedly throws his still lit cigarette away. It lands in a puddle of petrol near a car and causes an explosion. Oscar and Lucinda, occupants of the car, are burnt. Oscar dies. Lucinda, after hospital treatment for her burns, is discharged.

Discuss Bernie's criminal liability.

How, then, should this answer be structured? As suggested above, the first thing you must do *in your head* is to identify the legal issues (using the techniques referred to earlier). In this instance, it means identifying the offences with which Bernie will be charged and any defences that are relevant to these charges. Use these potential charges to structure your answer. In so doing, pay attention to the fact that the question contains two paragraphs, which implies that they are two distinct sets of events which may be handled separately for the purposes of legal analysis and thus for the purposes of your answer. It is perfectly legitimate to split your answer as follows: Bernie and the Cashier (the set of events in the first paragraph); Bernie and Oscar, and Bernie and Lucinda (the set of events contained in the second paragraph). However, don't overdo this: it is possible to over-organise and split up your answer into useless sub-headings which mask interrelationships and which give it a disjointed appearance.

There follows a very basic plan for the above question, to which we will add more detail in due course. While it may not be ideal, it is a sensible means of structuring your thoughts and using it will help present your material to good effect.

Bernie and the Cashier:

Under this heading you would write about the offences which you think Bernie has committed against the cashier.

Your *thinking process* might be something like this:

Possibly s. 18, OAPA 1861, intention to cause GBH (depending on whether tea is hot, problems with *mens rea*); and, more likely, s. 20, OAPA 1861 (maliciously inflicting (a) a wound, or (b) GBH); or s. 47, OAPA 1861 (assault occasioning ABH).

Bernie and Oscar:

Under this heading you would write about the offences you think Bernie has committed against Oscar.

Your *thinking process* might be something like this:

Murder? No. Doesn't have necessary *mens rea*; Manslaughter? Yes. Which type?

Bernie and Lucinda:

Under this heading you would write about the offences you think Bernie has committed against Lucinda.

Your *thinking process* might be something like this:

Possibly s. 20, OAPA 1861 or s. 47, OAPA 1861; possibly arson with intent to endanger life or being reckless as to whether life is endangered (s. 1(2), Criminal Damage Act 1971: aggravated arson).

At this stage you are half way there. You have compartmentalised your answer. All you need do now is fill in the boxes. How? Having isolated the parties take each one separately. Then apply what is sometimes referred to as the 'IRAC method':

I   Issue (with which crimes may the defendant be charged?).

R   *Rule of law* (the *actus reus* and *mens rea* of the crimes). For example, if the offence is murder, state clearly the law on murder, going through the *actus reus* and *mens rea*, all the while supporting what you write with authority (statutes, case law and, where appropriate, academic opinion).

A   *Application of the law to the facts*. Although this aspect is not at all straightforward, it is nevertheless very important, and it can make the difference between an average answer and a very good one. In applying the law to the facts, you must learn to look at both sides of the dispute. For example, in a criminal law question you should use the facts to show how the prosecution will try to demonstrate that the defendant comes within the parameters of the offence(s) as established in the relevant principles. To show that you are aware that there is always another way of looking at the facts, you should also argue how counsel for the defendant would try to demonstrate that the defendant does not fall within the definition of the crime, or, if he or she does, that a valid defence is available.

C   *Conclusion*. Often the problem question with which you will be faced will be set in such a way that the issues are very finely balanced. Don't be put off, however, by the fact that there is no 'right' answer – if there were right answers to all legal disputes, there would be no need to pay for lawyers to give advice. When asked to jump one way or the other, lawyers tend to describe the position they have chosen as the 'better view'. You can do the same. However, do not merely state conclusions; try to make sure that they are supported by reasoned argument. If necessary, outline any difficulties which might lead you to qualify the advice/answer given (e.g., not enough facts).

To summarise: state the issue; suggest the offence with which the defendant will be charged; identify the governing law; apply it to the facts (e.g., stating the arguments for both the prosecution and the defence); and lastly, end with a conclusion.

There are no doubt other structures – or variations on this one (see, p. 77) – and if you can think of another good one, use it. For the moment, we will use the first heading to illustrate the processes involved in filling out the answer according to the suggested technique:

Bernie and the Cashier:

Bernie (B) could be charged with s. 20, OAPA 1861 or s. 47, OAPA 1861. Section 20 contains two distinct, but related charges. First, unlawful and malicious wounding; and, secondly, unlawfully and maliciously inflicting GBH. The *mens rea* for both offences is found in the term 'maliciously'. *At the very least*, the defendant must foresee the risk of some harm occurring. However, he need not foresee serious harm resulting, i.e., he need not foresee the wounding or the infliction of GBH. It is irrelevant therefore to establishing the *mens rea* of s. 20 that the wounding was accidental provided the battery was intentional or reckless. This was established by the Court of Appeal in *Mowatt* (1967), and was recently confirmed by the House of Lords in *Savage; Parmenter* (1992).

The *actus reus* of the first charge is a 'wounding'. Although it need not be a serious cut, there must be a break in the continuity of the whole skin. An internal rupturing of the blood vessels is not a wound: *JJC (a minor) v Eisenhower*. It has long been established that there cannot be a wounding unless the wound results from an assault. Assault in this context definitely means a battery. See *Beasley* (1981, CA).

The *actus reus* of the second charge contained within s. 20 is 'inflicting GBH'. GBH means 'really serious harm': *DPP v Smith* (1961, HL). 'Really' adds nothing to 'serious harm': *Saunders* (1985, CA). Although there is authority for the proposition that 'inflicting' in s. 20 requires a technical assault (or a battery) as a prerequisite for a successful conviction (see, *Clarence*), any ambiguity would seem to have been resolved by the House of Lords in *Wilson* (1984), relying on the Australian case of *Salisbury*, where it was held that an 'assault' was unnecessary.

Prima facie, both s. 20 charges are sustainable. On the facts, it can be argued that by throwing the full cup of tea in the cashier's face, B foresees the risk of some harm – at least a battery. He need not foresee the harm which actually results. It would seem, therefore, that B has the requisite *mens rea* for a s. 20 offence. Further, since the inner and outer layer of the cashier's skin has been pierced, an injury within the meaning of 'wound' has been sustained by the cashier; and given that this resulted from a battery (throwing the liquid at the cashier – so that the requirement in *Beasley* (above) is satisfied – the *actus reus* of 'wounding' would seem to be established. Alternatively, provided the tea was hot – causing scalding – it could be argued that GBH was inflicted. A conviction on indictment on either count could result in five years' imprisonment.

B might also be liable under s. 47, OAPA 1861, assault occasioning actual bodily harm (ABH). ABH was defined by the court in *Miller* (1954, CA) as any hurt or injury calculated to interfere with the health or comfort of the victim. Trifling injuries do not, however, constitute ABH (*Miller; Chan Fook* (1994, CA)). It would appear that by throwing the cup of tea at the cashier, B did occasion (cause) ABH. The *mens rea* of s. 47, which is found in the case law, is intention or recklessness to cause at least a technical assault or battery, i.e., it is not necessary for B to intend or foresee the higher standard of harm, ABH: *Roberts* (1971, CA); confirmed by *Savage; Parmenter* (1992, HL). Intention bears its ordinary meaning throughout the criminal law: *Moloney* (1985, HL), *Hancock & Shankland* (1986, HL). Recklessness here probably means *Cunningham* recklessness or subjective recklessness (I foresee the risk, but carry on regardless): *Savage; Parmenter*. If B did not intend a technical assault or battery (which he probably did), he certainly seems to have been subjectively reckless as to the results of his acts: he foresaw the consequence that some harm, albeit slight, would result from his conduct, but carried on nevertheless. Absent a defence, B is liable on indictment for up to five years' imprisonment.

Points to note

(a)   The IRAC method has been adopted. The first charge alleged is s. 20 (I). The *mens rea* and *actus reus* of the crime have been set out (R). Both the *mens rea* and *actus reus* have been applied (A). Lastly, a conclusion has been reached (C). The same approach has been employed with respect to s. 47.

(b)   Start with the most important *relevant* crime first, then work down. If, however, you start with a s. 18 charge, eventually you will run into a dead end. For example:

Bernie and the Cashier

Bernie could be charged with s. 18, OAPA 1861. The *actus reus* of this offence is 'causing GBH', which means 'really serious harm': *DPP v Smith* (1961, HL). 'Really' adds nothing to 'serious harm': *Saunders* (1985, CA). The *mens rea* of s. 18 is intent to cause GBH. Intention in this respect bears its ordinary meaning: *Moloney* (1985, HL), *Hancock* (1986, HL). If the tea was merely warm, it is unlikely that GBH would have been sustained. However, if the tea was very hot, scalding would constitute GBH according to *Smith*. The problem is that even if the tea was boiling hot, Bernie does not appear to intend serious injury to the Cashier. [**Normally you are given a hint concerning the defendant's state of mind, e.g., the defendant says something like: 'I thought it was on the cards'**] Therefore a s. 18 charge, if brought, will be unsuccessful.

What you have written is, of course, basically correct, but you have said what Bernie is not liable for, rather than what he is liable for. The emphasis is wrong. If you must talk about s. 18 here, try the following:

A charge of s. 18, OAPA 1861, for intent to cause GBH, is unlikely to succeed because, even if the tea was scalding hot, Bernie does not appear to have the requisite *mens rea* (i.e. intention) to establish the offence. Bernie could, however, be charged with s. 20, OAPA 1861 or s. 47, OAPA 1861 [**then discuss these charges**].

This is a more promising start to your answer, since it indicates to the examiner that you know exactly why s. 18 is irrelevant and what the relevant charges should be. If the question has more issues than you can cover in the time allotted, there is no need to go all the way down to technical assault or battery, unless, that is, you are running out of ideas.

(c)   Sometimes it will be appropriate first to set out all the law relating to a charge (i.e., the *mens rea* and the *actus reus*) and then go on and apply it to the facts of the problem (e.g., s. 20 above). However, this need not always be the case. Note that in the above answer (see p. 17 in particular dealing with s. 47), the *actus reus* is set out first and then applied, after which the *mens rea* is set out and then applied. There are no established conventions on which way round it should be done, or whether the *actus reus* should be discussed before *mens rea* or vice versa. In fact, it doesn't really matter (but see, p. 26) provided the material is set out clearly and concisely, and that it is competently and comprehensively applied to the facts of the problem.

(d)   Note how authority is used to support the propositions of law. This is a crucial aspect of what lawyers do – it is their hallmark – and it is fundamental that you employ and perfect this technique if you wish to score well in exams. There are ten authorities cited for the first set of facts alone. Of course, in the answer provided, not every proposition which is cited is supported by an authority, but very many of them are. In those instances where you do cite authority it is not necessary to write out the full citation of the cases (e.g., [1995] 1 All ER 123), it is enough to write down the name or part of the name and – if you can remember – the year and court in which the case was decided. Indeed, this could at times be crucial from the point of view of assessing the precedential value of the decision.

3.   GETTING THE BALANCE RIGHT

Although some problem questions may test a student's all round legal knowledge of a subject, often they emphasise certain aspects of an issue (or issues).

A.   Offences/Defences

Since the question about Bernie (above) concerns offences rather than defences (has he any defences? – see later, at p. 38), you should concentrate most (all?) of your efforts on the offences. However, sometimes it is clear that although defendant may be charged with an offence, he has available to him a perfectly credible defence. Be logical. Address liability-creating factors first *then* move on to defensive strategies. Very often the latter are difficult to evaluate in the abstract, and sometimes they are impossible. For example, some defences (e.g., provocation and diminished responsibility) are available only to a charge of murder, so it is not relevant to discuss such defences until you have established that the defendant is to be charged with murder and why.

Question

Alan, Bill and Charles, who are all drama students, live together in a flat. On the afternoon of 27 June, when the results are released, it becomes clear that all three have failed one particular course option: 'Genre and Significance in Twin Peaks'. They suspect that Dr Death, the course tutor, has marked them unfairly. Alan, who has been in receipt of medication from his doctor to calm his nerves, takes three valium. This is just slightly in excess of the dosage which his doctor has prescribed. Bill, who is already pretty drunk, takes out his hip flask and drains it of its strong alcoholic contents. Charles meanwhile is getting more and more agitated and is muttering to himself that he 'hates tomatoes'.

Bill suggests that they go and see Dr Death in his room 'to sort this thing out once and for all'. Bill opens the door without knocking. Dr Death, who is with a colleague, is startled. He goes towards the three young men and offers them his handshake. Unfortunately, Bill thinks that Dr Death is trying to punch him, so he pushes his tutor against the wall. Alan then takes out his cigarette lighter. Some exam scripts which are sitting on the table grab his attention and he sets them ablaze. He then runs out of the room shouting 'fire, fire!'. Charles, meanwhile, picks up a letter opener and, unleashing a blood curdling yell of 'I hate tomatoes', stabs Dr Death's colleague in the eye, killing her instantly. Bill is horrified.

Discuss the criminal liability of Alan, Bill, and Charles.

Since the above question is primarily designed to test a student's knowledge of criminal defences rather than offences, your answer should reflect this bias. So, for example, the real issues in the above question are: intoxication/ diminished responsibility/insanity/self-defence. You should be able to work this out from the facts given: intoxication (hip flask – drunk); diminished responsibility/ insanity (acting irrationally – 'I hate tomatoes'); and self-defence – 'Bill thinks that Dr Death is trying to punch him'). Of course, to talk about these defences you must come up with some offences, but for the purposes of this question these are the side-issues. The point is, you have only a limited amount of time (usually 45 minutes) in the exam to answer the question, so when it comes to making sacrifices, sacrifice the detail on the offences so that you can spend more time on the defences.

Answer

Alan (A) will be charged with s. 1(2) and (3), Criminal Damage Act 1971 (aggravated arson) **[discuss this, following the rules identified earlier]**. He may seek to rely on the defence of intoxication (through alcohol or drugs). Self-induced (or voluntary) intoxication is available as a 'defence' if the defendant's intoxicated state amounts legally to insanity (*Beard* (1920, HL), *per* Lord Birkenhead). It is also a defence to specific intent crimes (*Beard*), but not to basic intent crimes (*Caldwell*, 1982, HL). Since, according to *Caldwell*, s. 1(2) is a basic intent crime, A could not plead voluntary intoxication. However in the light of the decision in *Hardie* (1984, CA) A may be afforded a defence where intoxication is self-induced otherwise than by alcohol or dangerous drugs. This is the case here: A becomes intoxicated by way of a non-dangerous drug (valium) i.e., one that is not normally liable to cause unpredictability or aggression. The fact that he takes more than the prescribed dose of the drug does not preclude him from relying on the defence. The crucial issue is whether he was reckless in taking the drug in the first place. It is unclear whether recklessness in this context is subjective or objective, but since the Court of Appeal in *Hardie* derived support from the decision in *Bailey* (1983, CA), it would seem that subjective recklessness is required i.e., the defendant must have foreseen the risk that the drug would make him unpredictable, aggressive, or incapable of appreciating risks to others, but have taken it nevertheless. Since A takes valium (a soporific drug) prima facie he has a defence available to him. And because he has only taken a dosage 'slightly in excess' of what the doctor has prescribed, it seems likely that a jury would not find him subjectively reckless in taking the pills. If A's plea is successful he will receive a complete acquittal.

Bill (B) could be charged with battery **[a s. 47 charge is unlikely given that the recent Crown Prosecution Service, Charging Standards, 1994, require extensive bruising, minor fractures etc., before such a charge is thought appropriate]**. He will seek to raise the 'defence' of mistaken self-defence. Despite the fact that self-defence is governed by the common law, the question of what amounts to reasonable force is the same as under s. 3, Criminal Law Act, 1967 (see: *McInnes* (1971, CA)). The first issue to be addressed is whether *any* defensive action is necessary/justified, and, if it is, whether the force used was reasonable. However, the position is different where the defendant mistakenly believes that force is necessary, when in fact it is not. In such a situation the defendant will have a defence if he honestly and genuinely, albeit unreasonably, mistook facts which, if true, would justify him using reasonable force in self-defence (*Williams, (Gladstone)*, 1984, CA, confirmed by *Beckford*, 1988, PC). Applying this to the problem, it could be argued that B does honestly and genuinely, albeit unreasonably, believe that self-defence is necessary and justifies pushing Dr Death against the door. If this version of events were upheld, it would turn what was, prima facie, an unlawful battery into lawful self-defence, and B would secure an acquittal.

However, the rules are more stringent where the mistake is a drunken mistake. There is authority to the effect that a defendant cannot rely on *any* type of mistake made when drunk (*Fotheringham*, 1989, CA; *O'Grady*, 1987, CA; *O'Connor* (1991, CA)). It is submitted, however, that this is probably a misreading of these cases. Provided the mistake is of the type which a sober person in those circumstances would have made (i.e., it is a reasonable mistake) then the defendant would be entitled to a defence. Since we are told that before seeing Dr Death, B was already 'pretty drunk' and that he goes on to drain his hip flask of 'its strong alcoholic contents', it would seem that the principles relating to drunken mistake would apply. But even if the mistake need only be that of the reasonable, sober person, it is unlikely that B would have a defence. It would seem unreasonable for B to mistake Dr Death's handshake for a menacing act which required defensive measures. B is, presumably, in a highly stressed and emotionally charged state following news of his recent exam failure and his drinking will, no doubt, have added to his state of confusion. It would seem, therefore, that B will be liable for the offence of battery. Since battery is a basic intent crime (*Majewski*, 1977, HL), and in view of the principles outlined above, a defence of voluntary intoxication will not be available to him.

Charles (C) will be charged with murder **[discuss]**. Counsel for the accused may wish to raise the issue of C's unfitness to plead (which relates to C's state of mind at the time of the trial). However, assuming C is fit to plead, Counsel will seek to raise the defences of diminished responsibility and/or insanity (both, relating to C's state of mind at the time of the alleged crime).

The law on diminished responsibility is governed primarily by statute: s. 2, Homicide Act 1957. It is only a defence to murder (s. 2(1)). The defendant alleging diminished responsibility must prove on the balance of probabilities that:

(i)   he has an 'abnormality of mind', meaning a state of mind so far removed from that of ordinary human beings that the reasonable man would term it abnormal: (*Byrne* (1960, CA), *per*, Parker LCJ)

(ii)   that his normality of mind arises from causes specified in the legislation (e.g., it is induced by disease or injury); and

(iii)   that his abnormality of mind, so caused, substantially impaired his mental responsibility ('substantially' is to be given its ordinary meaning: (*Lloyd* (1995, CA)).

It is irrelevant that the defendant knew that what he was doing was wrong and that it was premeditated: *Matheson* (1958, CA). The issue is one for a jury, although psychiatric evidence is admissible to help it reach a decision. A successful plea will result in a manslaughter verdict and sentencing will, therefore, be at the judge's discretion.

It seems likely that C would fall within the first and third limbs of the defence (see, above). A reasonable person would probably conclude that C's state of mind *at the time of the crime* (indicated by his speech, actions, and expert testimony) was abnormal. In addition, his abnormality would appear to have 'substantially impaired' his mental faculties – again borne out, most significantly, by the nature of his acts – mistaking a person for a tomato. However, C will find it more difficult to establish that his abnormality of mind arose from the causes specified in the legislation. His best hope would be that it was caused by inherent causes – e.g., that he was abnormally prone to stress, exacerbated by the pressure of exams and the fear of failure. The courts often interpret these causes liberally.

Since a successful diminished responsibility defence is nonetheless capable of resulting in life imprisonment, it may be wiser for C to plead not guilty by reason of insanity. The law on insanity is governed by the 1843 M'Naghten Rules, which are applicable to all crimes. The issue here involves consideration of the defendant's mental state at the time of the crime. According to the *M'Naghten Rules* it will be for Charles to prove, on the balance of probabilities, that he was labouring under a defect of reason (see: *Clarke* (1972) – there must be an inability to reason) arising from a disease of the mind (i.e., an internal factor, see, *Bratty* 1963, HL; *Sullivan* 1983, HL; *Burgess* 1991, CA) so as not to know the nature and quality of his acts or that they were wrong. The issue is one for a jury, although psychiatric evidence is admissible to help them.

Notwithstanding the narrow application of these rules, C's plea of insanity could well be accepted. Although the facts are not specific on this point, it is entirely plausible that C is suffering from a defect of reason which arises from a disease of the mind. Moreover, it would appear that by mistaking Dr Death's colleague for a tomato he is unable to comprehend the nature and quality of his acts, thus jumping the last hurdle necessary for the ingredients of the defence to operate. Where insanity is accepted as a defence to a murder charge, the judge has no choice but to make a hospital order: Criminal Procedure (Insanity) Act 1964, s. 5(3), as substituted by the Criminal Procedure (Insanity and Unfitness to Plead) Act 1991, s. 5.

Points to Note

Generally

Despite its length, the answer is not complete. There are other issues worth mentioning and, if you have time, expanding upon. For example, is Bill liable for burglary – s. 9(1)(b) style? Has he entered a building as a trespasser and then formed the intention to inflict or attempt to inflict GBH? Since burglary is a specific intent crime to which voluntary intoxication may be a defence, this would have been an interesting issue to raise. In addition, parts of the answer need to be qualified. For example, it is not strictly correct to imply that the burden of proof is always on the accused, since there is an exception: s. 6, Criminal Procedure (Insanity) Act 1964. Still, your answer does not need to be exhaustive in every detail – tracing the broad outlines of a subject will usually suffice.

Specifically

(a) Many students are especially weak when it comes to setting out the relevant rules and principles in relation to criminal defences. Often they adopt what will be referred to here as the 'soft centre approach'. For example, in the above question concerning C's liability, they will rightly discuss diminished responsibility, but the answer will usually go something like this:

> Charles may wish to plead diminished responsibility, which is a state of mind so abnormal that the reasonable man would say so. This was established in *Byrne*. Diminished responsibility is only available on a murder charge. If the defendant succeeds, the judge has a discretion on sentencing, so the defendant might receive life anyway.

What can we say about this answer? The most important point to note is that, despite its rather garbled form, the principles which have been mapped out in it are basically correct. There is even authority, and in the right place too. However, it will not score many marks in the exam. Why? Well, as has been pointed out, it is not enough to cite principles that are correct. They are necessary, but they are not sufficient. The principles need to be set out within some sort of coherent framework *and* they need to capture the essence of the defence, and the above answer achieves neither. The most glaring omission (which goes to the essence of the defence, but at the same times provides the framework around which to weave the answer) is the failure to say that diminished responsibility is governed primarily by statute: s. 2(1), Homicide

Act 1957. This point is absolutely crucial, because the statute lays down the main rules with respect to the operation of the defence, albeit that they are supplemented by judicial decisions. By using the statute as a 'peg' for your answer, you gain a ready-made framework. You can then set out the relevant rules in a logical order (abnormality of mind, specified causes, substantial impairment, and so on). Indeed, this common failure of students to point out the obvious is part of the wider principle, mentioned earlier, that you must assume that the examiner knows scarcely anything about the subject.

Incidentally, don't raise a defence unless the defendant has a *credible* chance of succeeding (i.e., there must at least be a hint in the question that it might apply). Neither should you write as one student wrote: 'the defendant could raise the defence of self-defence, but it will fail.'

Another good example of the soft centre approach arises with respect to the defence of provocation where two contrasting student answers, A and B, are outlined in response to the following question.

Question

Dan has big ears, a fact about which he is exceedingly sensitive. Recently, he has become interested in a classmate called Jenny, who sometimes comes to play with him in his garden. Dan's mother is building an extension to her house, and there are lots of bricks lying around. On a number of occasions, Victor, a boy from next door, has made fun of the size of Dan's ears while Jenny has been visiting. When this happens Dan usually runs away in tears. On one particular day while Jenny is visiting, Victor waves his hands behind his ears and pretends to take off like an aeroplane. Dan grasps the allusion. He walks over to the sand pit, picks up a brick and stoves Victor's head in, killing him instantly.

Discuss.

Answer A

Dan can plead provocation, but he must have lost his self-control. This is called the 'subjective condition'. But did Dan have 'cooling time' as in *Duffy*? In addition, a reasonable man must have lost his self-control at such provocation (the objective condition). In *Camplin*, the defendant was 15 years old. He was forcibly buggered by V, who started to laugh and gloat over his sexual triumph. The defendant lost his self-control and beat the man to death with a nearby chapatti pan. It was held that V's conduct amounted to provocation because the defendant had clearly been so angry as to have lost his self-control – and a reasonable boy of that age who had just been buggered might well have responded in a similar way. The reasonable man was to have the power of self-control to be expected of an ordinary person of the sex and age of the defendant, but also sharing such of the defendant's characteristics as was appropriate. Lastly, it must be shown that a reasonable man would have acted in the way the defendant did. **[It is hoped that these principles would then be applied to the facts.]**

Answer B

Dan (D) will be charged with the murder of Victor (V), which is a common law offence. The prosecution will argue that D threw the brick at V with intent to kill or cause GBH (*Cunningham* (1982, HL); *Hancock* (1986, HL)). Arguably, D could raise the partial defence of provocation, which is available on a murder charge only. If D's plea is successful, his sentence will be reduced from murder to manslaughter, and thus the judge will have a discretion over sentencing. If D raises the issue of provocation he only bears the 'evidential burden' of creating a reasonable doubt (i.e., he only has to make the defence of provocation a 'live issue' at his trial). By contrast, the Crown must prove beyond all reasonable doubt that there was not sufficient provocation to mitigate D's guilt to manslaughter.

The law governing provocation is partly statutory (s. 3, Homicide Act 1957) and partly common law. Provocation is the sudden and temporary loss of self-control, rendering D so subject to passion as to make him, for the moment, not master of his own mind (*Duffy* (1949, CA), *per* Devlin J). Before a successful plea of provocation can be established it must be shown that:

(a) D lost his self-control at the provocation (the subjective condition). If there is no evidence that this happened, the issue is withdrawn from the jury. An important question here is whether D had 'cooling time' (*Duffy* – desire for revenge is inconsistent with provocation). However, this must now be assessed in the light of a *dictum* in *Ahluwalia* (1992, CA) that cooling time does not negative provocation – it is an evidentiary matter. It is also possible that the provocation, while slight, would be the 'straw that breaks the camel's back'.

(b) A reasonable man would have lost his self-control at such provocation (the objective condition). The leading case is *Camplin* (1978, HL), where it was held that 'the reasonable man referred to [in s. 3] is a person having the self-control to be expected of an ordinary person of the sex and age of the defendant, but in other respects sharing such of the defendant's characteristics as they think would affect the gravity of the provocation to him' (*per* Lord Diplock). This is a question for the jury. However, a man is not entitled to rely on his 'exceptional excitability (whether idiosyncratic or by cultural environment or ethnic origin) or pugnacity or ill-will or on his drunkenness'.

(c) A reasonable man would have acted in the same way that defendant did. **[These principles should then be applied to the facts.]**

Which of these partial answers is best, and why? It should be clear that Answer A would not get an 'A' (even though it sets out the law on provocation first, before going on – it is hoped – to apply it to the facts), whereas Answer B is well on its way to obtaining a good grade. Notably, Answer A fails to discuss the crime of murder first; and then when provocation is raised it fails to locate the defence as deriving from common law or from statute law (or, indeed, as in this case, deriving from both). This is one of the first things you really should say, whether you are talking about an offence or a defence. If you like, it is one of the many bases you must touch if you wish to produce a polished answer. In developing your material on a particular point you should start off very broadly and then become more focused. You are producing a chart for the examiner to follow. He or she must be able to see the overview as well as the detail. The fact that s. 3, Homicide Act 1957 is not mentioned is a very grave omission, and is particularly so given that every law student should know that s. 3 plays a fundamental part in the law of provocation. In addition, Answer A is not exactly bristling with authority and, although some correct principles are mentioned, the answer is a bit 'thin' on the law. Lastly, the case of *Camplin* is handled in a rather pedestrian manner. Of course, Answer B is also far from perfect. For example, if B had 'cooling time' then the defence would fall at the first hurdle, and the other principles that you have outlined would lose relevance. You must be careful here. If there is a lot in a question, it might be wiser to write out the first paragraph and then the first limb of the test (i.e., the subjective condition) and then apply that limb to the facts. Since you could advance a good argument that D did have 'cooling time', you could close your discussion and move on to the next issue. However, if provocation is the only (or a major) issue in the question posed, either set out your material as in Answer B, or, if you have worked through the material stage by stage as suggested in this paragraph, say something like 'If on the other hand, it is found that D does not have cooling time, then . . .' and then proceed to write about the remaining two hurdles.

Clearly, with respect to cooling time, there is Lord Taylor LCJ's very important *dictum* in *Ahluwalia* to consider. Although this could be mentioned (as it has in Answer B) when setting out the relevant legal principles, it would also have been appropriate to have kept it in reserve – for when you are applying the law to the facts.

Answer B (and A) should also have considered whether the defence of infancy applied. There are facts which certainly warranted the issue being *raised*, even if it were ultimately to be dismissed. For example, you are told that they (i) were classmates (significant, but not decisive) and (ii) 'played' together.

(b)   Handle with care material which is mainly statutory (e.g., provocation and diminished responsibility). Avoid copying out the statute verbatim where you are provided with a statute book in the exam; instead paraphrase your material (see the earlier answer in relation to diminished responsibility). By contrast, where the law on a point derives from the common law, try to be as precise as possible (see, e.g., the earlier discussion of insanity). By doing so you will be able to demonstrate your knowledge of the law rather than your ability to copy material from one book to another.

(c)   You will note that in most of the above examples the principles relevant to the defence are set out first and then they are applied to the facts of the situation. This is a very safe way in which to marshall your material. For a start, it is very clear when it comes to marking the answer. Also it is a relatively straightforward operation to perform in the heat of the exam. However, it is not the only way in which to handle the material and it is not necessarily the best. Interweaving discussions of the law and fact may, on occasion, produce a more satisfactory answer, and will help vary the style of your approach (for more on this, see the contract section at p. 78).

(d)   By this stage, it may have struck you that presenting your material as suggested could require an alteration in the way in which you take notes. For example, when you read a case on some aspect of criminal law you must know exactly the crime charged, the ingredients of the crime, the particular question which the judges were seeking to answer, and the process(es) by which they arrived at that answer (i.e. the reasoning). It may also be helpful to jot down any problems to which the decision gives rise. So if you were taking notes on the *Caldwell* case you might write:

The defendant was charged inter alia with s. 1(2), Criminal Damage Act 1971, the ingredients of which are 'intending . . . to endanger the life of another or being reckless as to whether the life of another would be endangered'. The question the court had to decide involved one particular *mens rea* element: the meaning of the word 'reckless' as used in the section (subjective or objective?). The majority opinion (given by Lord Diplock – Lords Keith and Roskill concurring) held that objective recklessness sufficed, i.e., a person is reckless if:

(a)   he does an act which in fact creates an obvious risk; *and*
(b)   when he does the act he either –

(i)   has not given any thought to the risk *or*
(ii)   knows of the risk and carries on regardless.

Their reasoning was as follows:

Recklessness is not used as a term of art, but is to be understood in its 'dictionary' sense, i.e., 'careless, regardless, or heedless of the possible harmful consequences of one's acts'.

* * *

The dissent (given by Lord Edmund-Davies, Lord Wilberforce concurring) strongly disagreed with the majority for the following reasons [**read the judgment, and outline these reasons**].

Problems with the decision? The injustice of cases such as *Elliott* v *C (a minor)* (1983) 77 Cr App R 103 (where defendant lacked the *capacity* to appreciate risks) etc.?

This perhaps over-simplifies matters, because some cases stand for a number of propositions (e.g., *Caldwell* is also relevant in relation to the law on intoxication). Nonetheless, it gives you some idea of what you should be looking out for. Don't transcribe huge passages from the law report to your note-book. Put everything in your own words (except, of course, important quotations which you want to memorise for exam purposes). That way you will be forced to think more about what you are studying and it will probably help you to remember the material. One last (important) point. Cases are not only important in terms of outlining the 'tests' – the appropriate legal standards by which to assess liability/the conferral of rights (see pp. 37–38) – they are also a useful source of material with which to criticise the law (read a minority judgment: see, pp. 107–108)).

(e) It is common for student answers to contain some facetious remark relating to the facts of the question (e.g., in the above question on Alan, Bill and Charles, something about 'drama students'). Please desist. Such remarks are rarely as funny as you think they are and it makes your answer seem unprofessional.

(f) You may also have noticed the length of the Alan, Bill and Charles answer. In particular, it may have struck you as impractically long. It is, of course, important that your answer is comprehensive in terms of identifying the main issues while at the same time being as concise as possible in discussing those issues. However, it is unusual for a short answer to score a very high mark. That being said, examiners are well aware of the time constraints you are working under, so your answer does not need to be exhaustive. Although you do need to give the appropriate slant to your answer, if you do so by ignoring all together other aspects of the question you will undoubtedly be penalised, even though the material you have covered has been well presented. This is simply another way of saying that you get more marks for covering everything quite well than some things brilliantly and other things not at all or poorly.

B.   Issue Within the Issue

Often the central issue within a problem question (the really difficult one the examiner wants you to identify and resolve) will be hidden behind other issues. For example, someone may die, and the 'ultimate' issue will be whether the defendant is liable for murder or manslaughter. You will show this by demonstrating that all the ingredients of the particular crime you have chosen are indeed present. However, rather than gliding over all these ingredients, the examiner may expect you to focus on one particular issue, even though you must cover the others as well. In other words, the part of the question the examiner really wants you to focus on is not so much to do with the ultimate issue (which must nonetheless be discussed) but more about what will be called here the 'issue within the issue' – that is, some particular ingredient which must be established in order to resolve the ultimate issue. Causation illustrates both the 'issue within the issue' point and another problem to which we shall return later – that of stamping some sort of coherent order, or categorisation, on an apparently amorphous set of propositions.

Question

Anne and John dislike one another. One day Anne hits John over the head with a plank of wood. John falls to the ground, concussed and in need of hospital treatment. On the way to the hospital, another vehicle, driven by Nicky, collides with the ambulance, which was stationary at traffic lights. On his arrival at the hospital, the stretcher on which John is lying is dropped. He dies a week later. There is evidence that a blood clot sustained from the beating was exacerbated by the crash and the accident on the stretcher.

Discuss Anne's criminal liability.

Clearly the main issue here is whether Anne will be liable for John's death, either on a murder charge, or on a charge of manslaughter (gross negligence or unlawful and dangerous act – you must always specify the type of manslaughter with which you have charged the defendant). Whatever the charge, all of the elements will have to be proved. On the basis of either charge the *actus reus* (which is the same in both instances) will have to be proved (i.e., causing death). In other words, although on the face of it the issue is about Anne's liability for murder or manslaughter, the real issue (the 'issue within the issue') is whether Anne caused John's death, or whether there is a break in the chain of causation which absolves her of criminal liability for J's death.[1] Most students do not seem to realise that 'causation' is part of the *actus reus* (e.g., result crimes constitute an 'act' in 'legally relevant circumstances' which 'caused' the prohibited result).

Again, do not jump in. Your material must be set out in some sort of sensible order. Start off with the charges and then work through the problem. There is a plausible case for murder (Anne appears to intend to cause GBH), so start with the *mens rea* of murder. If the *mens rea* is not clear (and there is no indication in the question that it is), try the *mens rea* of the relevant manslaughter charges. You will definitely find sufficient *mens rea* to establish manslaughter. Given that the *actus reus* for murder and manslaughter is the same, you can take both together (assuming you have demonstrated the *mens rea* of murder).

Answer

* * *

To do so, it must be shown that 'A' was not only the factual (or 'but for') cause of the incident, but that she was also the legal cause (i.e., her actions amounted to a 'significant contribution' outside of the *de minimus* principle: *Pagett* (1983, CA); *Cheshire* (1991, CA). Legal causation is based on 'remoteness of consequences' and so the question arises whether there has been an independent intervening act – a *novus actus interveniens* – which will break the chain of causation as in *Jordan* (1956, CA) (on the basis that the doctor's treatment was 'palpably wrong'). However, in *Smith* (1959, CA), *Jordan* was distinguished and was said to be a case on special facts. Thus, apart from a completely overwhelming event, the courts have demonstrated a distinct reluctance to hold that an intervening act exists (see: *Smith; Cheshire;* and *McKechnie* (1992, CA)). **[Apply these principles to the facts.]**

---

1. Of course, other non-fatal offences against the person would be relevant if causation for murder/manslaughter was not established.

Students often expect a 'right answer' to a problem on causation, but more often than not no such thing exists. Just make sure that you discuss the problem sensibly, outlining the law and making plausible arguments based on the facts. If this still seems unhelpful, remember to err on the side of caution: very few events will break the chain of causation. It is also worth noting that this answer reduces the relevant law to a set of propositions (i.e., some order has been brought to bear on the authorities).

C. Tailor Answers to the Question Asked

It is not uncommon for students to misunderstand or carelessly ignore what exactly it is they are being asked to do by the examiner in the problem posed. At the end of every problem (usually on a separate line) you will be asked to respond to the collection of events which constitute the problem question. In criminal law problems you are generally asked to 'Discuss the criminal liability of the parties', or simply to 'Discuss'. Here you are not expected to act on behalf of one particular side. It may help, for example, to think of yourself as being in the position of a judge. Occasionally, however, you may be asked to advise one of the parties, Ms Smith (in which case you should not advise Ms Jones), or simply to 'Advise the parties' (in which case you should advise Ms Smith, Ms Jones, and anyone else who is involved in the problem scenario). Although it is necessary to consider arguments which go against your client, you are nonetheless obliged to present your client's arguments in the best possible light: good advice always takes account of counter-arguments and overcomes them. Very often students produce a general outline of the law, rather than advising the parties specified.

4. Analysing the Rules of Law

A. Resist the Temptation to be Led by the Cases

We saw earlier how students often begin answers by identifying and writing about cases with similar facts. However, this is not just a tendency in introductions – rather it represents a misguided *method* by which to analyse and present the relevant rules of law. That such a method permeates many student exam answers should come as no surprise, since law courses generally tend to stress the importance of learning cases. It is only natural, therefore, to expect students to write answers that reflect this bias. The following examples show how some pitfalls can be avoided.

Question

Dotty goes to the bowling alley one evening, to get away from her nagging husband. Liz, the repair person, is fixing some machinery at the end of one of the lanes. Dotty, who is in a state of great stress owing to her domestic problems, decides to roll a bowling ball down the alley, just to give Liz a fright. Fortunately, the ball misses Liz, but unfortunately it hits and breaks part of the machinery which Liz was trying to fix.

Discuss.

Answer A

[Could be attempted ABH; but not attempted assault (assault is a summary offence, an 'attempt' applies only to an indictable offence); criminal damage contrary to s. 1(2), Criminal Damage Act 1971. The partial answer below focuses on the recklessness aspect.]

In *Caldwell* it was established that recklessness in this context means objective recklessness. So where the defendant creates an obvious and serious risk and carries on regardless, or gives no thought to the risk when a reasonable person would have, that is objective recklessness. In *Elliott* v *C* it was held that the defendant's characteristics should not be taken into account. In that case C was a schoolgirl of below average intellect. She had been out all night and had had no sleep. Upon entering a garden shed, she found some white spirit and set the shed alight. It was held that she had created an obvious risk, and although it might not have been obvious to her it would have been obvious to the reasonable man; therefore she was reckless. In *Bell*, the defendant suffered from stress psychosis. He used his car to destroy the gates of a Butlins holiday camp and was charged with criminal damage. He argued that because of his stress psychosis he did not appreciate the risk. It was held that although he may not have recognised the obvious risk the reasonably prudent bystander would have. In *Sangha*, it was held that even if the defendant were an expert it would make no difference in assessing whether the risk was obvious.

* * *

Answer B

* * *

For the purposes of criminal damage contrary to s. 1(2), Criminal Damage Act 1971, objective recklessness will suffice (*Caldwell* (1982, HL)). A person is reckless in this sense if:

    (a)   he does an act which in fact creates an obvious risk; *and*
    (b)   when he does the act he either–

        (i)   has not given any thought to the risk *or*
        (ii)   he knows of the risk and carries on regardless (*Caldwell*; *Lawrence* (1982, HL)).

In applying this test, the defendant's characteristics are not taken into account (*Elliott* v *C (a minor)* (young backward girl who lacked sleep); *Bell* (1984, CA) (stress psychosis); *Sangha* (1988, CA) (expert)). The test is whether a reasonably prudent bystander would think there was a risk (but compare Lord Keith's *dictum* in *Reid* (1992, HL)). **[Apply to the facts.]**

It should be clear without too much explanation that partial Answer B is better than partial Answer A. Although there is nothing that is 'wrong' in the latter, it is too pedestrian. In particular, it reads like a list of cases, all of which basically say the same thing: The defendant's characteristics will not be taken into account when determining whether she was objectively reckless. In addition, the material is not as clear as it might be. Partial Answer B is, by contrast, clear and concise. It reduces the cases of *Elliott* v *C* (1983) 77 Cr App R 103, *Sangha* [1988] 2 All ER 385, CA, and *Bell* [1984] 3 All ER 842, CA, to one single, simple rule (mentioned above) and cleverly draws attention to the fact that there are *dicta* in *Reid* (1992) 95 Cr App R 393, HL, which in certain circumstances – apparently not present here – signal a retreat from this position.

Lastly, students often talk about a plaintiff or a defendant using X case to support their argument. For example, in talking about the lacuna they sometimes write something like: 'The defendant could use the *Shimmen* case to counter the argument that he failed to give any thought to the risk. In that case . . . ' Again, there is nothing 'wrong' with this mode of expression, but it could be misleading (in *Shimmen* (1987) 84 Cr App R 7, the defendant merely minimised the risk; he did not rule it out) and the point could be made more elegantly. For example, you might write:

> The defendant could argue that he 'falls' within the so-called lacuna in the objective recklessness test (i.e., that he foresaw the risk but ruled it out). This argument was raised and rejected in *Shimmen*, where the court held that defendant had merely minimised the risk rather than ruled it out. However, the existence of the lacuna has been explicitly endorsed by the House of Lords in *Reid*. . . .

Stamp your authority on the cases, do not let them lead you.

B.   Answer the Question on the Law as it is, not as it Ought to be

In general, problem questions do not require an evaluation of the merits of legal rules or an explanation of the rationale behind any particular rule(s). Rather, they are intended to test your ability to apply legal principles to complex factual situations. A critique of the law is more appropriate in an essay question, which often specifically asks you to criticise the existing law and to suggest reforms. Thus even if the law you are asked to apply is unjust, or out of date or inappropriate, it is perhaps advisable that you refrain from using problem questions as a platform for change. For example, in a s. 20, OAPA 1861 question dealing with a 'wounding', it would not be a high priority – though not wrong – to put forward an argument that, given advances in medical science, the wounding must amount to serious harm (see, Clarkson & Keating, *Text & Materials on Criminal Law* (3rd edn, Sweet & Maxwell, London, 1994), at 562). Of course, where the law is unclear, or the fact situation is a novel one and is not directly analogous to previous cases, the underlying rationale of a rule may help you to work out whether it extends or should be extended to cover the fact situation in question.

C. Impose Coherence on Confused/Confusing Areas of Law

Certain areas of criminal law provide students with particular difficulties when it comes to exams, because of the apparently 'bitty' nature of the topic. One such area is the law relating to accomplices. Here we will focus on the special rules pertaining to joint unlawful enterprises (if you are somewhat unclear about the exact relationship between accessorial liability and joint unlawful enterprise you are in good company: see Law Commission, *Assisting and Encouraging Crime* (Consultation Paper No. 131) (HMSO, London, 1993), paras 1.13, 2.108, and 2.119). The question we want to address is how these rules – whatever their exact status is – might be set out as a 'neat package' for the purposes of answering an exam question (or part of a question) on the topic of 'joint unlawful enterprise'.

Very often when students approach an area of law, they are confronted with a vast number of decisions which, taken together, resemble islands of single instances, with no coherent principles by which to make sense of them. As a result, the students' task appears overwhelming. The danger is that students will allow the material to manipulate them rather than the other way round. The only solution to this problem is to seek to classify the cases, in order to make them manageable. This is an important skill for a lawyer to have, and it is invaluable in the context of exams. The most straightforward means of classification – and it is one to which we will return often – is to outline the general rule and establish exceptions to it. If the material is susceptible to this form of categorisation, it will instantly become more manageable from your point of view and more comprehensible from the examiners. However, in the answer produced below, a slightly different form of classification is attempted, based on the accomplice's *mens rea*.

Question

Sam and Tim plan an armed robbery on Vera, an elderly, wealthy widow who lives alone. The plan is that Sam will hold her prisoner with a knife at her throat while Tim steals her jewellery. The plan is executed, but after Tim has taken the jewellery Sam deliberately stabs Vera, killing her. Tim confessed that he realised that there was a risk that Sam (known to be unpredictable) might do that, but he had fervently hoped that it wouldn't happen and would never have gone along had he known that Vera would sustain more than fright and slight injury.

A partial answer is set out below, containing some of the principles relevant to joint unlawful enterprises. Again, the tendency when answering this sort of question is for students to 'jump in' too soon. Divide up the material in the ways suggested in this book. For the main part of the question – liability for Vera's death – it might be better to discuss Sam's liability first, and then to move on to Tim's. However, in relation to armed robbery, it would be perfectly acceptable to discuss Tim and Sam's liability together.

Answer

* * *

The following principles are relevant to Tim's liability for the incidental offence [**i.e., Vera's murder**]:

(a) if an accomplice to an offence has expressly or tacitly agreed to the commission of the incidental offence, the accomplice is also guilty of the incidental offence (*Chan Wing-sui; Ward; Hyde; Hui-Chi-ming*);

(b) if an accomplice to an offence has contemplated the commission of the incidental offence as a 'real possibility', the accomplice is also guilty of the incidental offence (*Hyde; Roberts*);

(c) if an accomplice has thought about the possibility of the incidental offence being committed, but has dismissed it as negligible, he will not have contemplated the offence as a 'real possibility' (*Chan Wing-sui*);

(d) if the accomplice has not thought about the possibility he will not be liable (*Anderson* v *Morris*); however, if the offence does not require foresight of the consequences that actually do result (e.g., manslaughter and s. 20, OAPA 1861) he will be liable.

[These should then be applied to the facts of the above problem.]

The objection might be raised that many of the above rules are not relevant – that the answer should select only those that are relevant (e.g., (d) is certainly irrelevant on this basis) and move on. There is nothing wrong with that type of approach, and done properly it will lead to good marks being awarded. However, the advantage of the above method is that it allows you to create a legal context against which to set out the facts. You are able to demonstrate your legal knowledge and explain why certain rules do not apply and which others probably do. This approach should not be taken to extremes, but it can be useful on some occasions.

In certain instances it may be difficult to work out the boundaries of a rule. If this is the case, it may be helpful to set out a number of different possible formulations of the rule, supported by authority. You could, for example, start first with the most liberal formulation of the rule and work through to the most extreme version (or vice versa).

D. *The Doctrine of Precedent and the Rules of Statutory Interpretation*

In presenting and applying the law on a particular topic, you must be aware of the importance of the doctrine of precedent. Thus, it is crucial that you appreciate the difference between *ratio* and *obiter*, and the possibility of distinguishing otherwise binding precedents, overruling, and so on. Failure to do so may lead to the application of a rule which does not necessarily represent an appropriate response to the question posed. An answer which shows no awareness of these important facets of the common law tradition will be penalised. By the same token, if the words of a statute are ambiguous, you must demonstrate that you know how the courts would seek to resolve the ambiguity (see, for example, the House of Lords decision in *Pepper* v *Hart* [1992] 3 WLR 1032, specifying when it is permissible to resort to *Hansard* as an aid to statutory interpretation).

The difficult issue of working out the *ratio* of a case and knowing which rule to apply in view of the existence of competing rules in different courts, is explored by considering a question on intention in relation to s. 18, OAPA, 1861. This is followed by a discussion of the issue of statutory interpretation in relation to strict liability offences. There are, of course, many other rules relating to statutory interpretation (and precedent), but since this is not the appropriate place to discuss them, you should consult one of the standard textbooks on legal method.

Intention

Perhaps one of the best (and arguably most difficult) examples in criminal law where the doctrine of precedent has been in issue, relates to the meaning of 'intention'.

Question

Sarah, a first year law student, does not like Dr Nofun, who is the Warden of her hall of residence. One night Sarah sets fire to the Warden's flat, causing Dr Nofun to jump from his upstairs window and, as a result, break his legs. When questioned by police as to whether she realised that her actions would have caused serious harm, she shrugs her shoulders and says, 'I suppose it was on the cards'.

Discuss.

Typical Student Answer

Could the defendant be charged with s. 18, OAPA 1861? Yes, I think she could. The *mens rea* is intention. In *Moloney* it was held . . . In *Hancock & Shankland* it was held . . . In *Nedrick* it was held . . . In *Walker & Hayles* it was held that . . . **[You would discuss attempted murder as well, and s. 1(2), Criminal Damage Act 1971.]**

As we saw earlier, it is bad style to present the cases in this sort of chronological fashion. First of all, the legal significance of the principles that you write down should be acknowledged. It is helpful, therefore, if you can say whether a particular principle is part of the *ratio* of the case or whether it was merely an *obiter dictum*, whether it was said by the House of Lords or the Court of Appeal etc., and, on occasion, it may be helpful to know who said it (i.e. *per* Lord . . .). It is also helpful if, when outlining the applicable rules, you present them in the form of a synthesis. For example:

Answer

* * *

Intention bears the same meaning throughout the criminal law: *Purcell* (1986, CA). In general, judges should not seek to define the meaning of intention for juries (*Moloney* (1985, HL), reaffirmed in *Hancock* (1986, HL), dealing with murder charges). However, in 'exceptional' cases some guidance might be necessary to help decide when intention can be inferred (*Moloney*). The leading case is the House of Lords decision in *Hancock*, where it was held that the greater the probability of a consequence occurring, the greater the probability that it was foreseen, and the more likely it was that it was intended (*per* Lord Scarman). In an attempt to clarify the law, the Court of Appeal in *Nedrick* (1986) said that intention could be *inferred* where the defendant foresaw death or serious injury as 'virtually certain'; and that where the defendant foresees the consequences for all practical purposes as 'inevitable', the inference will be 'irresistible'. However, it was held by the Court of Appeal not to be a misdirection where the judge directed that the jury could infer intention where the defendant foresaw death or serious injury as 'very highly probable' (*Walker & Hayles* (1990, CA) – although the court also said that the *Nedrick* direction should be given in the future).

Whether Sarah (S) foresaw the consequences of her actions (i.e. serious injury) as 'virtually certain', is difficult to ascertain. The difficulty arises in determining whether 'I suppose it was on the cards' equates with 'virtually certain', although, as mentioned above, it was not a misdirection to infer intention from facts which the defendant foresaw as 'very highly probable'. This would be perceived as a slightly less strict direction than 'virtually certain'.

Strict liability offences

Although by no means the only area where statutory interpretation is important, offences of strict liability provide a good example of the need, at times, to be aware of the importance of this aspect of answering a problem question. For example, in determining whether a statute creates a strict liability offence it is necessary to construe the statute in the light of a number of guiding principles of law. These principles were clearly articulated by Lord Scarman in *Gammon (Hong Kong) Ltd* v *Attorney-General of Hong Kong* [1985] 1 AC 1, PC:

(a)   there is a presumption of law that *mens rea* is required before a defendant can be held guilty of a criminal offence;

(b)   the presumption is particularly strong where the offence is 'truly criminal' in character;

(c)   the presumption applies to statutory offences, and can be displaced only if this is clearly, or by necessary implication, the effect of the statute;

(d) the only situation in which the presumption can be displaced is where the statute is concerned with an issue of social concern (e.g., public safety);

(e) even where a statute is concerned with such an issue, the presumption of *mens rea* stands unless it can also be shown that the creation of strict liability will be effective to promote the objects of the statute by encouraging greater vigilance to prevent the commission of the prohibited act.

In determining whether a statutory provision 'clearly or by necessary implication' rebuts the presumption that *mens rea* is required in respect of some particular element of the offence, the courts will endeavour to discover Parliament's intention by reference to:

(a) the words used in the statute (e.g., words such as 'knowingly', 'intentionally', and 'maliciously' clearly indicate that *mens rea* is required, but difficulties arise where the words used are words such as 'permitting', 'wilfully', or 'cause');

(b) extrinsic factors (e.g., the higher the maximum prison sentence, the less likely it is that the statute will be construed as creating a strict liability offence); and

(c) whether strict liability would promote the object of the provision (e.g., whether making the offence one of strict liability would encourage greater vigilance to prevent the commission of the prohibited act: *Lim Chin Aik* v *R* [1963] AC 160).

5. APPLYING THE LAW TO THE FACTS

Although we have already touched on the issue of applying the law which you have set out in your answer to the facts of the problem (see pp. 16–17), there are other considerations also worth bearing in mind.

A. *Mark out the Boundaries of Liability*

It might be helpful for some students to think of the *actus reus* and *mens rea* of a particular crime in the form of a Venn diagram, the boundaries of which are determined by the tests in the relevant cases or statutes. Each new case will alter the boundaries of liability, advancing them in some cases, and sounding the retreat in others. Showing that the defendant's actions fall within the *actus reus* is necessary, but not sufficient (except in cases of strict liability) for the offence to be established. Similarly, demonstrating that the defendant's mental state falls within the *mens rea* is again necessary, but not sufficient. When the defendant falls within both sets, criminal liability ensues – the ingredients of the crime are established. For example, the definition of murder is intention to kill or cause GBH. The *mens rea* is intention (to kill or to cause GBH) and the *actus reus* is the causing of death or GBH. The defendant must intend to cause death, and do so; or he must intend to cause GBH, and do so, with the result that death flows from it (within a year and a day). The rules and principles which define the *mens rea* and *actus reus* of murder mark out the limits of liability – they represent the appropriate legal standard for liability to ensue. You must use the facts to determine whether, once these limits have been drawn, the defendant falls inside (using facts which support the prosecution's argument) or, outside (using facts which support defence counsel's argument); or if he does fall inside, whether he has a defence. In other words, in applying the law to the facts you are assessing whether the appropriate legal standards have been met. A well-devised question will give you scope to present the arguments for and against liability, although often the facts tend to point in one direction.

Consider the earlier question about Bernie (see pp. 14–15). You may recall he was charged with ss. 20 and 47, OAPA 1861. There are plenty of facts that would seem to place him within the 'boundaries of liability' established by ss. 20 or 47; but you may also have wondered whether he has a defence. Certainly most laypeople would say that he does – after all, he is 'mentally subnormal'. However, this is really a red herring in terms of establishing criminal liability. Why? First, Bernie drives a car, and, secondly, he is capable of realising that he has been short-changed. Therefore, he can't be *that* mentally subnormal. These factors go against him successfully raising a defence of, e.g., insanity. You would need to use these facts to indicate why his mentally subnormal state is irrelevant for the purposes of his criminal liability.

B.   Do Not Invent Facts

Sometimes an examiner deliberately (or perhaps inadvertantly)) leaves out a fact(s) which you would need to know to express a view on the defendant's criminal (or tortious or contractual etc.) liability. If this is the case, note it and state its relevance. For example, in the question about Bernie and the cashier, the examiner does not inform us whether the tea is boiling hot, warm, or cold. It seems sensible to comment on this, but don't make too much of it. Try to avoid blaming the examiner for failing to clarify all the facts of the problem, for although the problem may have been badly set, it is best to adopt a diplomatic approach. Try saying something like 'on the facts of the question there is nothing to indicate that . . .' or 'on the facts it is not clear whether . . .'. In this way, you avoid impugning the examiner's competence; and it is, on the whole a more sensible strategy, since examiners often mean to leave certain facts vague to allow you more scope for argument. Do not, however, take this leeway as a licence to invent facts at will. For example, avoid saying, 'If Bill had done . . . then he would be liable for . . .'. Likewise, avoid any attempt to make up your own question: 'What if Bill had killed Dr Death? . . .'. There are, of course, instances when it may be appropriate to make certain assumptions in your answer. For example, in the question about Alan, Bill, and Charles (see p. 20), since you are not told what sort of harm Bill has caused Dr Death, you should tell the examiner that you are assuming that a particular type of harm (specify) has been sustained – thus leading to the charge of a relevant offence (specify) – and get on with explaining the defences which Bill has a credible chance of pursuing. In the answer given above, it has been assumed that a minor type of harm has been sustained, thus giving rise to liability for a battery unless a defence can be established. One last point: do not worry about issues of proof; take the facts as given.

C. The Same Rules Apply to Statutory Offences

Usually students experience great difficulty in answering problem questions involving statutory offences, especially property offences. However, the techniques are exactly the same: the crimes will be limited to those covered in the syllabus (usually seven or eight offences, the most important of which are theft, obtaining property by deception, and burglary). You will need to know the *mens rea* and *actus reus* elements of these offences, many of which overlap. So if the charge is theft, go through appropriation, property, belonging to another etc. However, remember that there will usually also be an 'issue within the issue' to deal with and so you will therefore have to give appropriate weight to that aspect too. The question below, for example, concerns whether Billy is liable for theft (but note also, following the recent House of Lords decision in *Gomez* [1993] AC 442, the applicability of the offence of s. 15, Theft Act 1968, obtaining property by deception). In addressing the 'issue within the issue' point (with the emphasis on appropriation), the answer sets out the relevant legal rules in a comprehensive and comprehensible fashion.

Question

Billy hears that people in the next street are moving house and are using the Sunshine Removal Company. He arrives early one morning in his own furniture removal van, pretending to be the Sunshine Removal Company, and starts loading furniture into his van (under the general supervision of the owner of the house). He then makes off with the furniture, only to be apprehended later that day by the police.

Discuss.

Answer

Billy could be charged with theft, which is the appropriation of property belonging to another with the intention of depriving the other of it (s. 1(1), Theft Act 1968). The *actus reus* of the offence is the appropriation of property belonging to another. Appropriation is defined in s. 3(1) as 'any assumption of the rights of an owner'. The question arises here whether an appropriation can take place with the owner's consent (or apparent consent). In *Lawrence* (1972) the House of Lords said that consent was irrelevant for the purposes of s. 3(1) (*per* Viscount Dilhorne). In that case there was said to be an appropriation notwithstanding the fact that V allowed the taxi driver to take money from his wallet. However, according to the later decision of the House of Lords in *Morris* (1984), there could not be an appropriation if the owner consented (see also, *Skipp* (1974, CA), and *Fritschy* (1985, CA)). Following decisions by the Court of Appeal in *Phillipou* (1989) and *Dobson* (1989) where the approach in *Lawrence* was favoured, the matter has been settled by the House of Lords in the recent decision in *Gomez*, where it was held that there could be an appropriation notwithstanding the owner's consent, provided that the consent was obtained as a result of a false representation. **[Apply to the facts.]**

If a sensible argument can be made that all the ingredients of theft can be established, then it would probably be a good idea to apply the above rules on appropriation to the material before going on to discuss the next ingredient. That way you keep bringing your material back to the question. However, if the question is somewhat 'light' on issues in general, you could find yourself 'exiting' from the question (closing off your answer) long before you get the opportunity to demonstrate the full breadth of your legal knowledge. For example, if appropriation could not sensibly be established and this were the first ingredient you discussed, you would have difficulty developing your answer on theft much further. Note that having identified the ingredient you wish to discuss, you are required to set out the relevant statutory provision first and then to flesh it out with the various holdings in the cases. Thus, in relation to 'appropriation', s. 3 is discussed and then further discussion/clarification is drawn from the cases (*Lawrence, Morris, Gomez*).

6.   WRITING STYLE

In presenting your material, your style of writing is important. Some students write particularly well. Their sentences flow smoothly, following on clearly one from another. Provided they have the right problem-solving technique, these answers are generally a pleasure to read. Others, however, write poorly. Either their sentences are too long, with too many clauses, or they do not follow logically. Remember, you are putting together an answer for someone else to read and understand. It is not the examiner's job to work out what exactly it is you are trying to say. Rather, it is your job to make clear what you are trying to say. If you have particular difficulties writing good prose, keep your sentences relatively short. Make sure that your ideas follow on logically from one another; and, perhaps most importantly of all, take complex ideas and try to simplify them.

Chapter 2

The Law of Torts

The purpose of this chapter is to extend the problem-solving approach used in chapter 1 to tort problems. Rather than simply repeating the advice which has been offered in the previous chapter, the aim here is to select examples from tort law which reinforce the earlier-mentioned techniques. Naturally, where differences or qualifications are required they are outlined. This chapter is, at times, also illustrative of more specialised 'micro' structures around which answers can be arranged.

In terms of technique, the link between torts and criminal law is particularly strong: '[j]ust as the criminal law consists of a body of rules establishing specific offences, so, the law of torts consists of a body of rules establishing specific injuries. Neither in one case nor the other is there a general principle of liability.'[1] Thus, self-standing (nominate) torts will have their own peculiar ingredients (albeit that some of these are unclear and evolving) in the same way that different crimes have their own *actus reus* and *mens rea* ingredients.[2] And these torts will have applicable defences just as crimes have applicable defences. A quick glance at the questions posed will reveal that the same basic patterns found in chapter 1 are played out repeatedly, except this time we are interested not in the defendant's crimes but in the torts she has committed – and against whom – and her defences, if any. As with criminal law, you should have a template, or grid, of some sort – either written down, or clearly thought out in your mind – categorising the different torts

---

1. Quoted in *Salmond & Heuston on the Law of Torts* (20th edn, Sweet & Maxwell, London, 1992), at p. 18.
2. It should also be noted that '[o]utside these nominate torts there are wrongs which are well known to exist but which have no compendious name; beyond these again are wrongs which may possibly be torts, but which it is impossible to say whether they are such or not.' See, *Winfield & Jolowicz on Tort* (14th edn, Sweet & Maxwell, London, 1994), at p. 54.

(negligence, *Rylands* v *Fletcher*, nuisance, defamation, assault, battery, false imprisonment and so on) and noting the various legal principles relevant to each. Again, it is assumed that you know these elements and can recall them easily. Make sure you have distinguished clearly in your mind the difference between these torts and issues like vicarious liability. The latter form of liability does not, of course, represent a distinct tort, it is instead a means by which some person can be held liable for the torts committed by another; in other words it is a means of displacing liability from one person to another (e.g., from the employee to the employer). Naturally your list should include any applicable defences.

The questions discussed in this chapter focus on liability in negligence, liability under the Occupiers' Liability Acts 1957 and 1984 and the Animals Act 1971, and liability in *Rylands* v *Fletcher* and in nuisance. (Incidentally, given that some crimes are torts (e.g., battery is a crime and also a tort), it is important *for exam purposes* to keep these two bodies of law separate and to remember that different rules apply, most obviously in relation to the standard of proof, but in many other significant respects as well.)

A word of warning about negligence is appropriate. Negligence is a self-standing tort – the tort of negligence – but it may also be relevant to the way in which other torts are committed (e.g., nuisance – see Stanton, *The Modern Law of Tort* (Sweet & Maxwell, London, 1994), at pp. 395–6) and, as we shall see in the next chapter, it is also a way in which contracts can be breached (see pp. 69–71). It is important to see the role of negligence in different contexts and to appreciate the variations in, and the overlap of, the rules which apply.

1. TACKLING A PROBLEM QUESTION ON THE TORT OF NEGLIGENCE

To sue someone successfully for the tort of negligence, the plaintiff must show *on the balance of probabilities*:

(a) that the defendant *owed* the plaintiff a legal duty;
(b) that the defendant *breached* that legal duty;
(c) that the breach *caused* the plaintiff damage;
(d) that the *damage* was not too remote.

(a) = DUTY; (b) = BREACH; and (c) and (d) = DAMAGE

If the plaintiff is able to show the above, then the defendant may wish to raise a defence (e.g., *volenti non fit injuria* (consent), or contributory negligence). It is probably worth mentioning that most defences relate to the plaintiff's conduct whereas liability (prima facie) depends on the defendant's conduct.

This, then, provides a framework – a 'micro' structure – around which a negligence answer could be presented. Whatever way your answer is structured – by issues, by parties, chronologically – these legal standards would have to be addressed in some sort of logical format. This should become clear from the answer to the following question:

Question

Alice, an elderly lady with poor eyesight, goes shopping one day in her local supermarket, Safeco. As she enters the store she is thinking about what to buy for her evening meal. Just inside the entrance there is a display of jam arranged in a pyramid. As Alice walks into the store she bumps into the pyramid, causing it to collapse. Many of the jam jars are smashed and broken glass ends up everywhere. Flustered, but unhurt, Alice continues with her shopping. Safeco lose jam valued at £400. Dirk, who is at the other end of the store, is choosing a frozen turkey at the time of the accident. He thinks that the noise is a bomb explosion and suffers severe shock. Dirk refuses to shop in Safeco since the accident, as the memories are too traumatic for him.

Bill, a 16-year-old petty criminal, has recently been sentenced to do 100 hours' community service in Safeco but receives a small amount of pocket money and his meals while on duty. While collecting abandoned shopping trolleys, Bill begins to fool around. Suddenly he loses control and pushes the line of trolleys into Alice's path. Alice suffers from a fragile bone condition and as a result of the accident sustains multiple fractures.

Discuss.

Before looking at the suggested answer, it might be helpful to consider for a moment a possible framework which you could use in tackling the above question. The legal issue (which in every case is negligence) is placed in brackets:

> Safeco v Alice (negligence)
> Dirk v Alice (negligence)
> Alice v Bill/Safeco?/Home Office? (negligence)

Then within each heading you can apply the duty, breach, damage formula.

Answer

Safeco v Alice
The first issue is whether Safeco (S) can successfully sue Alice (A) for the common law tort of negligence. To do so, S must show *on the balance of probabilities*:

    (a)   that A *owed* S a legal duty of care;
    (b)   that A *breached* that legal duty;
    (c)   That the breach *caused* S damage ('but for' causation); and
    (d)   That the *damage* was not too remote.

In *Donoghue v Stevenson* (1932, HL), Lord Atkin laid down two principles which determine the existence of a duty of care: foreseeability and proximity. The test of foreseeability is an objective one and is based on whether a reasonable person in the defendant's position would have foreseen that his actions would adversely affect others. Proximity refers to whether the defendant would have expected his actions to affect a particular person or class of persons. Recent cases have added an additional limb to this test: the imposition of the duty must be 'fair, just and reasonable' (confirmed by the House of Lords in *Marc Rich* v *Bishop Rock Marine* (1995)). Applying these principles to the problem it would appear that A owes S a duty of care. A reasonable person in A's shoes should have been able to foresee that by acting carelessly she might adversely affect others. There is also sufficient proximity, since it is reasonable to foresee that S would be amongst that class. Finally, the imposition of the duty would seem to be 'fair, just and reasonable' in the circumstances.

In addition to the existence of a legal duty of care, it must also be shown that A breached her duty of care to S. 'A' must exercise the care of an ordinary person (*Roberts* v *Ramsbottom* (1980)). The test is objective (*Nettleship* v *Weston* (1971, CA)). Omitting to do something that a reasonable person would do, or doing what a reasonable person would not do, amounts to a breach of care. On the facts, A would appear to have breached her duty of care since by thinking of what she would have for her evening meal instead of concentrating on where she was going, she fails to live up to the standards expected of a reasonable person. It is no defence for her to allege that she is shortsighted: *Nettleship* v *Weston*, where a learner driver was held to the standard of a normal driver. However, it was emphasised by the Court of Appeal in that case that the 'higher' standard was justifiable because the defendant was compulsorily insured. The courts may, therefore, be more generous in their interpretation of reasonableness in the case of an uninsured defendant.

Next, we must consider whether A's breach was the factual cause of the damage sustained by S (the 'but for' test: *Barnett* v *Chelsea Hospital*; *Wilsher* v *Essex* (1987, HL)). This would not be difficult to show on the facts. S must also show that A's negligence was the legal cause, i.e. the issue of whether the damage was too remote. In *The Wagon Mound* (1966, PC) it was held that damages could only be recovered for the type of harm that was reasonably foreseeable, albeit that the precise series of events that produced the harm was not foreseen (*Hughes* v *Lord Advocate* (1963, HL)); neither does the extent of the damage need to be foreseen (*Hughes*). In other words, a tortfeasor is liable to an unlimited extent for all losses caused by his act which are reasonably foreseeable. The breaking of the jam jars would have been a foreseeable consequence of A's actions. S would, however, only be permitted to claim for consequential loss, and not for any pure economic loss (*Spartan Steel* v *Martin* (1972, CA)). Thus, S could recover for the £400 worth of jam and for the cost of cleaning it up. However, S could not claim for lost profits for the fact that Dirk does not shop there anymore.

It would seem therefore that S has a fairly solid case against A. The latter's only defence might be to claim that S was contributorily negligent, resulting in a reduced award of damages (see *Copps* v *Miller*, where a motorcyclist had his damages reduced by 10% for not wearing his helmet). Here there is a good argument that S is to some degree responsible for its own misfortunes by virtue of the fact that it stacks, in the form of a pyramid, easily breakable jars near the entrance to the supermarket.

Dirk v *Alice*

The tort of negligence allows claims to be made for mental as well as physical or pecuniary harms (*McLoughlin* v *O'Brian* (1983, HL); *Alcock* (1992, HL)). The defendant may therefore wish to sue A for the nervous shock occasioned by the breaking of the jam jars. Broadly, the same 'hurdles' as discussed in the above section of the answer apply (i.e., duty, breach, damage). According to Lord Wilberforce in *McLoughlin*, the following questions are relevant to a claim in negligence for nervous shock: (i) was the plaintiff within the class of persons whose claim should be recognised? (ii) what was the geographical proximity of that person to the accident? and (iii) by which means was the shock caused? Given the restrictive nature of this test (see: *Alcock*), it might be thought that the defendant's claim will fail (he doesn't seem to fall within the class of persons and he doesn't see the accident). However, it is still possible for him to recover where he is in fear of immediate physical injury to himself. *Dulieu* v *White* (1901) has not been criticised on this point (*McFarlane* (1994)). As the facts show, the defendant was in fear of injury to himself, albeit that he was mistaken about the nature of the noise. He has, therefore, at least an arguable case for damages for shock.

Alice v *Bill/Safeco/Home Office*
'A' may sue B in negligence for the injuries she sustains as a result of her collision with the shopping trolley. Again the principles set out in *S* v *A* (above) are relevant. It would seem clear that B owes 'A' a duty of care and that the duty has been breached. Equally, it seems clear that 'but for' the breach A would not have sustained her injuries. The crucial issue here, however, seems to be whether the extent of her injuries was foreseeable, in that A suffers from a fragile bone condition of which B was unaware. Although in *The Wagon Mound* it was held that only reasonably foreseeable damage could be compensated, it was enough to foresee the occurrence of a particular *type* of harm; it was not necessary to foresee the *extent* of that harm. It could be argued that B should have foreseen the type of harm that could be sustained (broken bones) from his conduct. In any case (i) it is reasonably foreseeable that an old lady would have a fragile bone condition; and (ii) B must take the victim as he finds her: (*Smith* v *Leech Brain* (1961)). On the latter basis, A's fragile bone condition would be irrelevant for the purposes of imposing liability on B; it would not break the chain of causation.

If Bill has no money or no insurance, A may wish to sue S, who may be vicariously liable in negligence for B's actions. To do this, A needs to establish that B was S's employee (which seems unlikely on the facts). The parties' own labelling of the relationship is not conclusive (*Ferguson* v *Dawson* (1975, CA)). No single fact is decisive. Factors taken into account include the degree of control exercised by the employer, the degree to which B is part of S's organisation, the nature of payment, and the nature of the employment contract (*Ready Mixed Concrete* (1968)).

* * *

A might also consider suing the Home Office (or the relevant Governmental body) for B's tort. The courts have been reluctant to attribute liability for the acts of third parties (*Smith* v *Littlewoods* (1987, HL); *Topp* v *London Country Bus* (1993, CA)), but in exceptional circumstances, for example, where the defendant has control over the third party who causes the harm and the third parties actions are reasonably foreseeable (*Dorset Yacht* 1970, HL), a duty will be owed. Such a duty is unlikely to arise under the facts in the problem, since the Home Office lacks a sufficient degree of control over B and in any case the harm caused is arguably not reasonably foreseeable.

Indeed, even if a prima facie duty were established, it is likely that the duty would be negated by considerations of policy.

Analysis

Generally

In the cold light of day, this answer may seem 'nothing special', but in the heat of the exam it will require a lot from you in terms of recall, organisation and application; and in the eyes of the examiner it will stand out as an oasis in a desert – a clear, concise, and authoritative approach to an awkward multi-party problem question. This is not to say that the answer is beyond improvement. No doubt there are all sorts of qualifications or further explanations which one could make, but it is along the right lines: pairing up the parties, identifying the relevant issues, elucidating the relevant rules and principles, applying them to the question so as to reach reasoned conclusions. This, you will recollect, follows closely the so-called IRAC method (I = Issue; R = Rule(s) of Law; A = Application; and C = Conclusion) discussed in chapter 1, and forms the basis of the problem-solving approach used here. For example:

[Parties]	Dirk v Alice
[Issue]	The tort of negligence allows claims to be made for mental as well as physical or pecuniary harms (*McLoughlin* v *O'Brian* (1983, HL)); *Alcock* (1992, HL). The defendant may therefore wish to sue A for the nervous shock occasioned by the breaking of the jam jars.
[Rule]	Broadly, the same 'hurdles' as discussed in the above section of the answer apply (i.e., duty, breach, damage) **[see the part of the answer dealing with *Safeco* v *Alice*]**. According to Lord Wilberforce in *McLoughlin*, the following questions are relevant to a claim in negligence for nervous shock: (i) was the plaintiff within the class of persons whose claim should be recognised? (ii) what was the geographical proximity of that person to the accident? and (iii) by which means was the shock caused? Given the restrictive nature of this test (see: *Alcock*), it might be thought that D's claim will fail (he doesn't seem to fall within the class of persons and he doesn't see the accident). However, it is still possible for D to recover where he is in fear of immediate physical injury to himself. *Dulieu* v *White* (1990) has not been criticised on this point (*McFarlane* (1994)). As the facts show, D was in fear of injury to himself, albeit that he was mistaken about the nature of the noise. He has, therefore, at least an arguable case for damages for shock.
[Application]	As the facts show, defendant was in fear of injury to himself, albeit that he was mistaken about the nature of the noise.
[Conclusion]	He has, therefore, at least an arguable case for damages for shock.

The point of the answer is not to produce a blueprint for you to follow, but to show, by example, the *way* in which you can go about producing an answer which will do justice to your legal knowledge and at the same time enable you to score well in an exam.

Specific points to note

(a) *Issue identification and structure*   Since – as in all legal problems – we are trying to determine the rights and liabilities of the parties, the answer has focused on the tort committed by each of the 'actors'. The legal issue here, then, is who is liable in negligence and to whom?

(b) *Rule of law*   In addition to a good clear structure the answer does not shy away from outlining the relevant legal rules. In fact the law is set out clearly, using the 'micro structure' duty, breach, damage format. Since these elements are relevant to more than one area of the answer, it is permissible to refer back to some of the principles you have mentioned earlier if they are in fact relevant to the discussion you have embarked upon (for an example of this, see, *Dirk* v *Alice*, and *Alice* v B/HO/S). Most of the legal rules are supported by authority – over ten cases are cited. The variety of ways in which these authorities are handled is worth noting. For example, in one instance, the case is mentioned and then the principle is outlined:

> In *Donoghue* v *Stevenson* (1932, HL), Lord Atkin laid down two principles underlying the existence of a duty of care: foreseeability and proximity (confirmed by the House of Lords in *Marc Rich* v *Bishop Marine* (1995)). **[The addition of a more recent authority allows a student to demonstrate in an abbreviated way that he or she is aware of the recent cases.]** The test of foreseeability is an objective one and is based on whether a reasonable person in the defendant's position would have foreseen that his actions would adversely affect others. Proximity refers to whether the defendant would have expected his actions to affect a particular class of person.

Again:

> In *The Wagon Mound* (1966, PC) it was held that damages could be recovered only for the type of harm that was reasonably foreseeable.

This may be contrasted with other examples where the principle is outlined and then the authority for the proposition is given:

> A must exercise the care of an ordinary person (*Roberts* v *Ramsbottom* (1980)).

> Next, we must consider whether A's breach was the factual cause of the damage sustained by S (the 'but for' test: *Barnett* v *Chelsea Hospital*).

It is permissible (and perhaps desirable) to support your proposition of law with more than one authority:

In addition, the courts are reluctant to attribute liability for the acts of third parties (*Smith* v *Littlewoods* (1987, HL); *Topp* v *London Country Bus* (1993, CA)).

Legal rules can be stated in the negative:

It is no defence for her to allege that she is shortsighted: *Nettleship* v *Weston*, where a learner driver was held to the standard of a normal driver.

or the list method can be used:

According to Lord Wilberforce in *McLoughlin*, the following questions are relevant to the claim in negligence for nervous shock: (i) was the plaintiff within the class of persons whose claim should be recognised? (ii) what was the geographical proximity of that person to the accident? and (iii) by which means was the shock caused?

Lastly, the case can be used as an example of the point the student wishes to make:

The latter's only defence might be to claim that S was contributorily negligent, resulting in a reduced award of damages (see *Copps* v *Miller*, where a motorcyclist had his damages reduced by 10% for not wearing his helmet).

Note also, how, when dealing with a new topic within the problem, the answer goes from the general to the specific:

The tort of negligence allows claims to be made for mental as well as physical or pecuniary harms (*McLoughlin* v *O'Brian* (1983, HL) **[general]**.

D may therefore wish to sue A [in negligence] for the nervous shock occasioned by the breaking of the jam jars **[specific]**.

Again, this is a way of introducing your material (i.e. the law). The general statement helps to locate your new paragraph on the 'legal map', while the specific statement gets you to the heart of the problem. Such an approach is both extremely clear and along the right lines for the purposes of presenting your material in terms of legal issues and principles.

   (c) *Application* In addition to issue-spotting, structuring your answer and outlining the law, it is necessary for the legal principles you have identified to be applied to the facts. The answer, again, demonstrates this:

Applying these principles to the problem, it would appear that A falls within this test and hence does owe S a duty of care, since a reasonable person in A's shoes should have been able to foresee that by acting carelessly she might adversely affect others.

In fact, the part of the answer headed *Alice* v *Bill* offers a good example of what was referred to in the criminal law section as the 'issue within the issue'. Clearly the 'ultimate' issue here is whether Alice can sue B, S, or the HO for the tort of negligence. However, this is both obvious and easy. What the examiner is really getting at is the 'issue within the issue', i.e. the more detailed – tricky – element(s) within the tort. The examiner knows that you will spot and discuss the ultimate issue, but he or she wants the bulk of the discussion to be on the more difficult part. Your application of the law to the facts must be sensitive to this point. For example:

> A may sue B in negligence for the injuries she sustains as a result of her collision with the shopping trolley. Again the above principles set out in *S* v *A* (above) are relevant [see the part of the answer dealing with *Safeco* v *Alice*]. It would seem clear that B owes A a duty of care and that the duty has been breached. Equally, it seems clear that 'but for' the breach A would not have sustained her injuries [that disposes of the general issue]. The crucial issue here, however, seems to be whether the extent of her injuries was foreseeable, in that A suffers from a fragile bone condition of which B did not know. Although in *The Wagon Mound* it was held . . . [here attention is focused not on the tort of negligence generally, but on the damage limb, and on only one particular aspect of it].

Again, as in criminal law – with *actus reus* and *mens rea* – there is no convention on whether, when applying your material to the facts, you should set out all the law on duty, breach and damage first and then apply to the facts, or whether you should set out each limb separately and apply. Much will depend on whether the examiner expects you to get over all the hurdles. Clearly, if no duty can be established there is little point in discussing breach and damage.

Confirmation of this type of approach – of setting out the law first and then applying it to the facts – can be found in the law reports. For example, Lord Goff's speech in the House of Lords decision of *Henderson* v *Merrett Syndicates Ltd* [1994] 3 WLR 761 at pp. 773–8, where his Lordship outlines and extends the principle in *Hedley Byrne* v *Heller* [1964] AC 465 (dealing with negligent misstatements) (pp. 773–7) and then applies it to the facts (pp. 777–8). See also Lord Denning's judgment in *Esso Petroleum* v *Mardon* [1976] 2 All ER 5 at pp. 14–16, CA; and for an even more obvious example see Lord Denning's judgment in *Seager* v *Copydex Ltd* [1967] 2 All ER 415, at pp. 417–8, CA.

(d) *Conclusion*   The answer argues towards a conclusion in each section. For example:

> *Safeco* v *Alice*
> S would, however, be permitted to claim for consequential loss only, and not for any pure economic loss (*Spartan Steel* v *Martin*). Thus, S could recover for the £400 worth of jam and for the cost of cleaning it up. However, S could not claim for lost profits from those customers it had to turn away while cleaning up. . . .

Sometimes (e.g., where the defendant has a defence) your conclusion will need to take account of defensive strategies. Again, as with criminal law, it is appropriate that defensive strategies are discussed only after having identified liability creating factors:

> The latter's only defence might be to claim that S was contributorily negligent, resulting in a reduced award of damages (see *Copps* v *Miller*, where a motorcyclist had his damages reduced by 10% for not wearing his helmet). Here there is a good argument that S is to some degree responsible for its own misfortunes by virtue of the fact that it stacks, in the form of a pyramid, easily breakable jars near the entrance to the supermarket.

2. OCCUPIERS' LIABILITY AND THE ANIMALS ACT 1971

Negligence liability in *Donoghue* v *Stevenson* and its offspring is concerned with establishing a common law duty of care in certain circumstances (e.g., nervous shock, negligent misstatement and so on). By contrast, in relation to occupier's liability, a specific duty of care is imposed by statute. Consequently, occupier's liability can be considered as a special type of negligence, governed by its own special rules.

Although liability for damage caused by animals can be established on the basis of ordinary tort principles (e.g., common law negligence), this is another area where statute law is particularly important, (Animals Act 1971). The following question highlights these issues.

Question

Jack owns a derelict plot of land which he intends to develop when market conditions are suitable. He has erected a fence around the site, upon which he has placed notices stating: ' Private property. Keep out. Anyone entering these premises does so at their own risk. All liability for any damage is hereby excluded.'

Local children have for some time been entering the plot through a large gap in the fence in order to play. Kylie, aged 10, was playing hide and seek on the plot when she sustained serious injuries as a result of falling through a rusted manhole cover which is obscured by undergrowth.

Following this incident Jack had the fence repaired. He allowed a stray mongrel dog to wander around the plot and fed it regularly. He hoped that the presence of the dog would deter intruders. He placed additional notices on the fence stating 'Beware of the dog'. Lenny, aged 17, was playing football against the fence when the ball was accidentally kicked over the fence onto Jack's land. Lenny climbed over the fence to retrieve the ball and was savagely attacked by the dog.

Discuss.

Answer

Jack's liability to Kylie

Jack (J) may be liable to Kylie (K) under the Occupiers' Liability Act 1957 (OLA 1957) or 1984 (OLA 1984). Since the duties created by both Acts are owed by 'occupiers', it must be shown that J fulfils this requirement. The test for occupier (a term which is not defined by either statute) is 'occupational control', though control does not have to be exclusive (*Wheat* v *E Lacon* (1966, HL)). Since J owns the plot of land and intends to develop it (he has control over it) he is covered. In addition, before either Act can be invoked, it must be established that J occupies 'premises', defined widely in s. 1(3), OLA 1957, to cover land and movable and immovable structures. Since J owns and is in control of the land, and all therein, including the rusted manhole cover – which might constitute a movable structure – there is a strong argument to suggest that he occupies premises. Again, for both statutes, injury must result from the state of the premises or from things done or omitted to be done on them. There is an argument that injury to K results from either ground: hidden dangers and J's failure to clear away the undergrowth from the manhole, so that people could see the potential danger. For a duty to be owed under the OLA 1957 it must be established that K was a 'visitor', i.e., a person who either (i) has the express permission of the occupier to visit the premises, or (ii) can be said to have an implied permission to be there (s. 1(1) OLA 1957). Although K does not have permission to be on the land as such, the law has generally been sympathetic to children in occupier's liability cases. At common law, a child could be upgraded to a visitor if there was either an allurement or an implied licence. For there to be an allurement there must have been something on the land that was both 'fascinating and fatal' (*Glasgow Corporation* v *Taylor* (1922)). Given that the plot was derelict – but for undergrowth – there would not appear to be an allurement. For there to have been an implied licence, it must be shown that J was aware of child trespassers and had taken no steps to keep them out (*Lowery* v *Walker* (1911, HL)). J should have been aware that children had, for some time, been entering the land and playing. There was a large gap in the fence which had not been mended. This, of itself, may be enough to establish an implied licence, in which case K would be a visitor and J would owe a duty to keep her safe for the purposes of her visit (which is to play: s. 2(2)). J must then do all that a reasonable occupier would do to help keep her safe.

An occupier has a number of defences available to a claim brought by a visitor under the OLA, 1957: (i) contributory negligence; (ii) consent or assumption of risk (s. 2(5)); (iii) exclusion of liability (subject to the Unfair Contract Terms Act (UCTA) 1977): s. 2(1) OLA 1957.

If K is deemed by the law not to have an implied licence to be on the land (as is entirely plausible), she will be viewed as a trespasser and therefore will be unable to rely on the OLA 1957. However, J may be liable under the OLA 1984 which applies to 'non-visitors' e.g., trespasses: s. 1(1)(a) OLA 1984 ('occupies', 'premises' 'things done and omitted to be done' are given the same definition as above). According to s. 1(3) of the Act, J owes a statutory duty of care to non-visitors if:

(a) he is aware of the danger and has reasonable grounds to believe that it exists;
(b) he knows or has reasonable grounds to believe that a non-visitor is in the vicinity of the danger; and
(c) the risk is one which reasonably requires the non-visitor to receive some protection.

It is unclear whether J was aware of the danger, and there is a plausible argument that he did not have reasonable grounds for knowing of its existence, especially since the manhole was covered. Similarly, the facts do not make clear whether he knew or had reason to believe that non-visitors were in the vicinity. However, it could be argued that the fact that J puts up a notice and erects a fence means that he does recognise the existence of some risk and it may mean that he was aware that non-visitors were, indeed, in the vicinity; the notice and the fence may have been his response to this knowledge. In addition, if J knew there was a hole in the fence it would be very difficult for him to deny the existence of a duty under s. 1(3). Certainly the risk – a hidden danger – is of the type one might reasonably expect would require the non-visitor to receive some protection.

If J is deemed to owe a duty, he must take such care as is reasonable in all the circumstances of the case to ensure that the non-visitor does not suffer injury as a result of the danger in question: s. 1(4) (i.e., relates to the *standard* of care owed). Although there is some degree of doubt as to the exact nature of the test to be applied (see Stanton, *The Modern Law of Torts*) it seems reasonable to assume that the court will demand a higher standard of care from a public corporation than from a homeowner. Factors taken into account when determining reasonable care include:

(a)   the seriousness and probability of injury – the greater the risk, the greater the precautions needed;

(b)   the nature of the premises;

(c)   the degree to which it was foreseeable that the non-visitor would enter them.

Surely it is highly foreseeable that children, especially, will enter a derelict plot and that they could injury themselves, albeit not seriously? A hidden danger – as in the problem – would increase the probability of injury, and therefore require that J take greater precautions. J's premises are in a bad state. The fence is in need of repair and parts of the plot are overgrown (greater chance of hidden dangers). It would seem, therefore, that J has not discharged his duty of care.

In certain circumstances, however, an occupier can discharge his duty by taking reasonable steps to (i) give a warning; and (ii) discourage non-visitors from incurring the risk (s. 1(5)). The notice would probably not suffice as a warning – something more would be needed. In any case, where the victim is a child (as here; K is only 10) a warning is unlikely to be enough. Although Jack fenced off the area, the fencing is defective, and therefore it is extremely unlikely that his attempts would be successful. In addition, the failure to the maintain the fence is probably the cause of K's injuries (distinguishing *Titchner* (1983, HL)).

According to s. 1(6), the occupier will not be liable where the non-visitor voluntarily assumes the risk. Since K is only 10, a plausible argument can be made that she is still a child and thus not capable of appreciating the risk. The same argument would probably apply in relation to the defence of contributory negligence.

The OLA 1984 makes no reference to the issue of whether an occupier can exclude or restrict her or his potential liability under the Act. If it is possible to exclude all duties (on the basis that all duties can be excluded unless statute says otherwise) then subject to common law rules (e.g., *contra proferentem*, where any ambiguity will be construed against the party seeking to rely on the exclusion clause) J will not be held to be liable to K. However, it could be that no duties may be excluded (or only some, e.g., it may not be possible to exclude the 'minimal' common law duties owed to trespassers by virtue of *Herrington* (1972, HL)) in which case J would have to place heavy reliance on s. 1(5) and (6) as defences. This is a very unclear area and the whole issue of whether it is possible to exclude one's duties remains an open question.

If J's duty can be excluded, the protections offered by the UCTA 1977 do not apply, since s. 1(1), UCTA deals only with the exclusion of liability for common law negligence and the duty owed under OLA 1957. It is worth nothing that the absence of any mention of the OLA 1984 in s. 1(1), UCTA 1977 would tend to support the argument that Parliament intended the OLA 1984 duty to be non-excludable.

J's liability to Lenny (L)

J may be liable to L under the Animals Act 1971. In accordance with the requirements of s. 2(2), liability can be imposed on anyone who *keeps* an animal which belongs to a *non-dangerous species*. A mongrel dog would be classified as non-dangerous, since it is an animal commonly domesticated in the British Isles (s. 6(2)). J is liable as keeper if he owns the dog or has it in his possession (s. 6(3)). Since he feeds the stray, this would probably be enough to bring him within the section, but in any case he has the dog fenced in, so clearly he has it in his possession. Basically, liability ensues if the keeper has actual knowledge (constructive knowledge will not suffice) that the dog had characteristics that would render it dangerous (s. 2(2)). It is again unclear whether all the requirements of the subsection are fulfilled. In particular there is little to indicate that J knew that the dog had any aggressive characteristics: he 'hoped' that it would deter intruders. The sign merely says 'Beware of the dog', not 'Beware: *Dangerous* Dog'. We are not told if the dog has previously attacked. On the other hand, J was using the dog as a guard dog, and a guard dog which was not aggressive would be pointless.

Even if s. 2(2) is satisfied, J will have a defence if the injury was wholly L's fault (s. 5(1)) (if it was partly L's fault then an issue of contributory negligence applies – see Law Reform (Contributory Negligence) Act 1945, ss. 10 and 11); if L assumed the risk (s. 5(2)) or if it was reasonable to keep the dog for the purpose of protecting property (s. 5(3)) (this subsection applies only if L is a trespasser, which would have to be established). It is arguable that all these defences apply: L is 17 and should know better (see *Cummings* v *Granger* (1977, CA)). However, s. 5(3) should now be construed in the light of the Guard Dogs Act 1975 (since it is likely that J has committed a criminal offence under that Act, it is unlikely that a court would hold what he has done reasonable for the purposes of s. 5(3)).

If J does not fall within s. 2(2), then he may be liable on the basis of ordinary negligence principles [**discuss the tort of negligence: duty, breach, and damage**].

Analysis

(a)   Again, at a general level, the answer is supported by a good, clear, tight structure: who may sue whom, and for what? Under each heading the relevant tort(s) is/are identified and the appropriate rules are set out. Subsequently, the rules are applied to the facts to reach credible conclusions in the light of possible defences and/or mitigating factors.

(b)   The question requires students to make good use of their *statutory* material by clearly setting out, and subsequently applying, the relevant law to the relevant facts. However, although the approach is essentially the same as that suggested for common law material (see pp. 37–38), there are nonetheless specific difficulties worth looking out for and helpful hints which can be followed to help resolve them. Since statutory material can often be complex, you should try to see whether it is possible to summarise the provision(s) in a line or two, by capturing the essence of the liability involved. An example of this in the answer can be found in relation to the Animals Act 1971:

> Basically, liability ensues if the keeper has actual knowledge (constructive knowledge will not suffice) that the dog had characteristics that would render it dangerous (s. 2(2)).

Having something like this to write down will prevent you becoming swamped by the complexity of the statutory provision(s) and will demonstrate to the examiner that you have been able to manipulate the material. Of course you do not have to formulate this sort of synthesis yourself, you may find it done for you in a textbook or an article.

It may, however, not be possible to reduce the complexity of a key statutory provision to a single sentence: for example, s. 1(3), OLA 1984. Nonetheless, in the answer, every effort has been made to simplify the subsection, by paraphrasing its essential elements (see also, chapter 1, p. 22 dealing with s. 2, Homicide Act 1957 (diminished responsibility)).

(c) The common law is not excluded unless a statute uses words that point to that conclusion. Therefore in many legal textbooks and articles the common law position on a particular issue is often considered first, with the statutory position being overlaid.[3] Thus, as a general rule you should outline the common law position first and then proceed to consider the effect of the statute on the area. Such an approach is, however, not appropriate with respect to the present question. Although the common law has some relevance, the Act provides extensive coverage for occupiers' liability and it is only in a 'filling in the gaps' sense that a discussion of the common law would really be necessary (e.g., in relation to 'occupiers', or in relation to excluding duties). So, if faced with the above question in an exam, you should focus on the statutory material first and merely fill in the gaps with common law principles. Needless to say, you should not discuss the common law position if it has in fact been totally overridden by statutory developments.

3. RYLANDS v FLETCHER/ NUISANCE/ NEGLIGENCE

Question

Alan operates a factory in Bristown in which he manufactures computer components. For the purposes of this work Alan keeps a stock of metal foil at one end of the factory. As a result of the door of the factory being left open, some of the foil is blown

---

3. But note, that although the statute might not have the effect of abrogating the common law on a particular issue, in a practical sense it will often mean that it is rarely resorted to because the statutory regime is clearer and less cumbersome.

out of the factory by a gust of wind. It lands on an electricity pylon owned by Branson Electrical Supplies plc, damages the pylon and causes a power cut in the area.

Celia operates a factory next door to Alan which manufactures plastic gnomes. When the power is cut off the production line ceases to operate and the electrical furnaces which process the plastic go off, cool and have to be cleaned out. The power remains off for the next 48 hours. Celia claims to have lost £10,000 profits as a result of these occurrences.

Delia, who was riding her moped past the factory at the time the foil was blown out, was struck by some foil, crashed the moped and was killed.

Discuss.

Answer

Alan's liability to Branson

Rylands v *Fletcher:* This is a strict liability tort (i.e., if the elements of the tort are satisfied it is irrelevant that the defendant has taken reasonable care to avoid the damage caused – albeit that certain elements seem to have a reasonableness component). Physical damage (as here) is covered by *Rylands*. The tort is not confined to claims between adjacent landowners (*Charing Cross* v *Hydraulic Power* (1913, CA)). There is English authority to suggest that even a non-occupier who has no interest in the land of any kind can invoke the rule (*British Celanese* v *Hunt* (1969), where damage occurred on a third party's land). Thus, the fact that Branson (B) is not an adjacent freeholder is irrelevant for the purposes of liability. B has a prima facie claim, even though it appears merely to have an interest in the pylons on the land, rather than in the land itself.

An action in *Rylands* v *Fletcher* will arise where there has been: (i) an escape; (ii) of a thing likely to do mischief; (iii) which has been brought on to the land; and (iv) has a non-natural use.

'Escape' for the purposes of liability in *Rylands* means 'escape from a place where the defendant has occupation or control over land to a place where it is outside his occupation or control' (*Read* v *J Lyons*, (1947) *per* Lord Simon). Applying this to the facts, there has been an escape: foil from A's factory (which was in his possession or control) has moved to a place where it is outside his occupation or control.

Whether there has been an escape of 'anything likely to do mischief if it escapes' (*Rylands*, *per* Blackburn J) is a question of fact. The 'thing' does not need to be dangerous *per se*; the issue is whether it is dangerous in the circumstances of the particular case. The defendant needs to have knowledge or means of acquiring knowledge of the dangerous propensity of the thing, i.e., was the thing brought on to the land known to be dangerous/mischievous? In addressing this issue the courts pay heed to the 'common experience of mankind' (*Crowhurst* v *Amersham* (1878)). It has been suggested by the writer of *Salmond & Heuston* that the courts are merely struggling with a version of whether the harm was foreseeable. It is irrelevant that all reasonable precautions were taken. Applying this to the facts of the problem, A must surely have known, or had at his disposal the means of knowing (his employees could have told him) that the foil had dangerous propensities were it not properly stored. Common sense would indicate this; the harm is foreseeable.

The dangerous 'thing' must have been brought on to the land, i.e., accumulated (as with the foil in the problem). The occupier will not be liable for anything naturally on the land. Consequently, landslides and other naturally occurring phenomena are not covered. In addition to accumulations there must be a non-natural use of the land. It must amount to 'extraordinary', 'exceptional' or 'abnormal' activity. Traditionally, it must not involve (i) ordinary use, or (ii) use for the benefit of the community (*Rickards* v *Lothian* (1913, PC)). A could argue that he comes within the decision in *British Celanese,* where it was held that the manufacture of electric components on an industrial estate did not constitute a non-natural use. However, the House of Lords has recently taken a more progressive approach towards this issue. In *Cambridge Water* (1994), it was held that the storage of substantial quantities of chemicals for industrial use was the 'classic' case of non-natural use of land. The fact that the activity would have benefited the community – by the creation of employment – was not sufficient to make the use natural. Applying this to the facts, A would seem to be liable, since, by analogy, the storage of metal foil would appear to be covered. However, the quantity of foil, and the purpose and manner of its storage, would need to be ascertained before a more reliable conclusion could be drawn (*Mason* v *Levy Auto Parts* (1967)).

Nuisance   An action in private nuisance is defined by Winfield & Jolowicz as 'an unlawful interference with a person's use or enjoyment of land, or some right over, or in connection with' (adopted with approval in *Read* v *Lyons* (1945, CA) *per*, Scott LJ).

Traditionally, two types of interference are recognised as being capable of giving rise to an action in nuisance (*St Helen's Smelting Co.* v *Tipping* (1865, HL)):

(a)   interferences with P's beneficial use of the premises (e.g., excessive noise: *Christie* v *Davey* (1893)); basically, the idea here is that the interference should substantially detract from P's comfort or enjoyment in the use of her premises; or
(b)   physical injury to the premises or to P's property situated on the premises, e.g., causing damage to P's land.

By leaving the factory door open and thus allowing the foil to be blown out of the factory, A would appear to have effected an interference on B on both grounds. The foil interferes with B's beneficial use of its pylon (i.e., to make profits; pursue its business interests); the foil also causes physical damage to B's pylon (this would probably be the better ground on which to proceed).

Not every interference is actionable – people must tolerate a certain degree of interference – it must be shown that the interference was unreasonable. Reasonableness is a question of fact. This is relatively straightforward where the interference results in physical damage to property (as here). Where, however, the interference relates to the enjoyment of the land, plaintiff must prove substantial interference, such that it would affect the reasonable person's comfort.

Even if there has been an unlawful interference, B may not have a sufficient legal interest in the land to allow it to sue. However, in line with modern authorities on this issue (e.g., *Khorasandjian* v *Bush* (1993, CA) – judicial willingness to accommodate an interest on the basis of any type of occupation or possession), it would seem that in all likelihood B does have a sufficient legal interest in the land.

Assuming B's action is successful it will be able to claim damages for any loss which is reasonably foreseeable (*The Wagon Mound (No. 2)* (1967, PC)). Therefore, in addition to the repair of the damaged property, business losses which result from the fact that the pylon has been damaged by the nuisance are recoverable (e.g., *Andreae* v *Selfridge* (1938, CA), losses caused to hotel owner as a result of a nuisance calculated by way of lost custom).

Negligence Liability may also arise in negligence [**discuss, in particular, whether there is a duty of care – difficult to argue foreseeability or proximity**].

Alan's liability to Celia

In accordance with the rule established in *Weller* v *Foot & Mouth Disease* (1966), Alan (A) will not be liable to Celia (C) in *Rylands*. In that case it was held that the Ps – cattle auctioneers – who suffered loss when sales of cattle were stopped due to an outbreak of foot and mouth disease, could not sue under the rule because *Rylands* did not provide a remedy for pure economic loss. Hence C will be able to sue under *Rylands* only if there was actual damage to her furnaces.

Liability may, however, arise in negligence, if it can be shown that A owed a duty to C (which would involve foreseeability of harm to her) and that A breached that duty (by falling below the standard of the reasonable factory owner). Nonetheless, there is still the problem of what damage C has suffered. If property damage can be established, C can recover for that damage and for any consequential economic loss (*Spartan Steel* (1973)). If the loss is purely economic, the law is reluctant to allow recovery (*Spartan Steel*), although *dicta* in recent cases suggest that a duty might exist not to cause the plaintiff such loss (e.g., *Marc Rich* (1995, HL)).

A's liability to Delia

Rylands v *Fletcher* A question mark still hangs over the issue of whether a plaintiff can claim for personal injuries under the rule in *Rylands* v *Fletcher*. There is authority in a number of Court of Appeal decisions that personal injuries may be recoverable (*Hale; Perry*). On this basis Delia (D) would appear to have a prima facie case. However, in *Read* v *Lyons* several members of the House of Lords were doubtful whether such an award was possible. The permissibility of an action may hinge on the paintiff's status: an occupier could claim for personal injuries, but a non-occupier could not. There is some support for this proposition in the Australian case of *Benning* (1970). If this rule were followed, D would be unable to claim for her injuries, since she is merely a passing motorcyclist and not an occupier of the land. The distinction, however, could be criticised as being arbitrary and is unlikely to be followed in the UK where, in any event, no case for personal injuries under *Rylands* v *Fletcher* has been recognised for nearly 50 years. D would therefore appear to be fighting an uphill battle.

Either negligence or public nuisance [**Discuss (briefly) either negligence (see *Hilder* v *Assoc Portland Cement* [1961] 1 WLR 1434 – football escaped into road knocking motorcyclist off – but unlikely), or public nuisance or both. But note, where there is already liability in *Rylands* or nuisance, liability in negligence would rank very low on your list of priorities.**]

Analysis

(a) It is clear from the answer that the issues here involve liability in *Rylands*, nuisance, and negligence (note that liability in negligence is capable of cropping up almost anywhere in a torts exam). Although the answer could have been structured on the basis of the issues/torts, again a split along 'party lines' was preferred. Had the issues/torts approach been adopted the flow of the answer would have looked like this:

Liability in Rylands v Fletcher

Alan's liability to Branson
> Ingredients of the tort
> Application to facts relating to *A* v *B*
> Conclusion

Alan's liability to Celia
> Apply the above ingredients to reach a conclusion

Alan's liability to Delia
> Apply the above ingredients to reach a conclusion

Liability in negligence

> *Alan's liability to Branson*
> Ingredients: duty, breach, damage
> Application
> Conclusion

Alan's liability to Celia
> Apply the above ingredients to reach a conclusion

Alan's liability to Delia
> Apply the above ingredients to reach a conclusion

Liability in Nuisance

Alan's liability to Branson
> Ingredients of the tort
> Application to facts relating to *A* v *B*
> Conclusion

Alan's liability to Delia
> Apply the above ingredients to reach a conclusion

Although under this structure you would minimise repetition of the relevant principles, it requires more of an 'aerial' view of the question, demanding more of you than the chronological / parties approach which has been heavily utilised by us. Nonetheless, it is a useful method and, if done properly, will allow you to score good marks.

(b)   The key elements which need to be shown are set out. Unlike with criminal law, you will notice that many of the ingredients of the torts alleged are unclear. This fact may be frustrating, but it need not be problematic from the point of view of sitting an exam, because it provides you with – as it were – more 'grist for your mill'. For example, in relation to the definition of 'non-natural use', there is some doubt as to exactly what this phrase means. The answer shows good awareness of this and the material is set out contrasting the 'traditional approach' with the House of Lords more 'progressive approach' in *Cambridge Water*. It is the later approach which is actually applied. Although the conclusion is reached that there is a non-natural use of the land, this conclusion is sensibly qualified by a request for more information as to the quantity of the foil and the manner of its storage.

(c)   You will note that there are a number of 'issue within the issue' points: for example, in discussing A's liability to C (in *Rylands*). Here the conclusion has been presented first, after which there is an explanation – supported by authority – of why the conclusion is justified. Similarly, in addressing A's liability to D there is a clear 'issue within the issue' point; namely, whether the plaintiff can claim for personal injuries under the rule in *Rylands* v *Fletcher*. The other ingredients need not be discussed – this is especially so since they have already been dealt with elsewhere in the answer. This section of the answer requires a fairly detailed knowledge of the nature of the harm capable of resulting in liability in *Rylands*. Note that the various possibilities are outlined and applied one by one. Here the context (that the law is uncertain) allows for criticism ('this distinction could be criticised . . .') and note also that this criticism is supported by an argument advanced in *Salmond & Heuston*.

Chapter 3

The Law of Contract

As with the previous chapter, the purpose here is to apply the problem-solving approach outlined in chapter 1 and developed in chapter 2 – this time to specific areas of contract law. In doing so, we again provide 'micro structures' around which to present answers. As before, we are interested in identifying legal issues, presenting the relevant law and applying it to the facts so as to reach reasoned conclusions. However, while the same techniques as outlined earlier are broadly applicable, there are some significant differences in emphasis. Unlike crime and torts, there are no longer easily definable categories of offences/torts and defences to provide 'ready-made' frameworks around which to build answers. Thus contract problems require us to modify slightly the problem-solving method we have so far employed. In this respect it will be helpful to pay particular attention to the following three points:

(a)   Generally, the first step in any contract question is to discover whether a contract exists, since an understanding of the legal issues stems from the existence of a contract. Some questions specifically focus on the issue of formation (e.g., the first two questions in this chapter). In other questions, however, it is clear that a contract has been formed; instead the examiner is interested in issues relating to the extent of the obligations owed and the performance of the contract (e.g., a question on exemption clauses, or frustration or breach). On other occasions, the contract will have been formed, but the legal issue(s), for example, relates to statements made before the formation of the contract which have induced one party to enter into it (as with misrepresentation). The point is: formation of the contract is central to any contract question, albeit that it is not the *focus* of all contract questions.

(b)   Insofar as there is a key with which to 'unlock' contract problem questions, it lies in addressing the various *statements* (written and oral) made by the different parties in the question posed. It is important, therefore, that you are able to categorise and assess the contractual significance of these statements and to outline any accompanying remedies (the first question below, about Zoe – involving contract formation – provides a good example of this process at work). The above proposition – that you should concentrate on statements – should not be construed too narrowly. The statements must be considered in their context: the status of the parties (i.e., their bargaining positions); the setting – formal or informal (e.g., after a long night of drinking and frivolity); the expressions or gestures of the parties; and so on.

(c)   As with criminal law and tort, a grid or template of some sort is again of use in helping you to spot issues; and since many students find it difficult to spot the issues in contract questions, an outline of the key aspects of your course may prove invaluable. At a very basic level, your outline might include: (i) formation; (ii) vitiating factors (mistake; misrepresentation etc.); (iii) terms of the contract (e.g., exemption clauses); (iv) breach; (v) remedies; and so on.

The topics covered in this chapter include formation, exclusion clauses, misrepresentation, and mistake.

1.   FORMATION

Questions on contract formation are standard fare in contract law exams. While conceptually they are usually straightforward, they are often 'bitty' and structuring your answer can at times be problematic.

Question

Zoe, a young ballerina with no head for business, needs £150 urgently to pay a bill. On Tuesday evening she discusses her problem with some friends, Julia and Kathleen. Julia suggests that she sell a valuable pair of antique ballet shoes that she recently inherited from her great aunt, a famous ballerina. 'All right,' says Zoe, 'I'm willing to sell them to either of you for £150. But you'd better post me a written acceptance by Friday morning.'

On Wednesday, Zoe meets Julia in the supermarket. Julia tells Zoe that she would like to buy the shoes, but has to talk to her father first, and that he is abroad until the weekend. 'Oh,' says Zoe, 'forget about that, there's no rush. Just give me a ring some time.'

On Thursday, Julia unexpectedly receives a large cheque from a fond uncle. She rings Zoe, but gets no reply. So she immediately goes round to Zoe's flat and puts a note through the door which reads, 'I accept your offer of the shoes. Herewith a cheque for £150.'

On the same day, Kathleen posts a letter to Zoe purportedly accepting the offer. But it is delayed in the post and arrives on Saturday.

On Saturday, Zoe discovers that the ballet shoes are worth £1,000.

Advise Zoe.

Answer

Issue I: Offer or invitation to treat?

Any obligation Zoe might have to hand over the shoes will stem from the existence of a contract which she has entered into. It will therefore need to be shown that what Zoe said constitutes an 'offer'. According to *Treitel*, an offer is 'an expression of willingness to contract on specified terms, made with the intention that it shall become binding as soon as it is accepted', i.e., the offeror must be prepared to implement his or her promise should the other person decide to hold him or her to it. The test is objective (*The Hannah Blumenthal* (1983, HL)), so there may still be a contract if, objectively speaking, the parties can be said to have agreed, even though there was not an express agreement. Where there is evidence that the person merely intends to start negotiations which may result in an agreement, s/he is said to make an 'invitation to treat'. So, for example, the display of goods in a shop-window (*Fisher* v *Bell* (1961)) or on the shelves of a self-service shop (*Pharmaceutical Society of GB* v *Boots* (1953, CA)) is an invitation to treat – in such cases the customer is deemed to make the offer. In Zoe's case, the words 'I am willing to sell to you . . . ' could, objectively speaking, be construed as an offer, since they indicate a willingness to be bound by certain terms as opposed to an attempt to start negotiations. In addition, she specifies the terms of the acceptance (written acceptance by Friday morning), even though certain aspects of the acceptance remain unclear (e.g., whether she will sell to the first to reply, or to the one who makes the highest offer).

Issue II: Does Zoe make a contract with Julia?

According to *Treitel* an acceptance is 'a final and unqualified expression of assent to the terms of an offer', which must be communicated to the offeror (*Holwell Securities* v *Hughes* (1974, CA)).

One possible interpretation of the events at the supermarket is that Julia makes a conditional acceptance of Zoe's offer (conditional on her father's agreement). On this basis there would be a contract and Zoe would be under an obligation to part with the ballet shoes. Yet such an interpretation seems strained and, objectively speaking, it is unlikely that a contract has been formed.

Another possible interpretation of what happens when Julia meets Zoe at the supermarket, is that what Julia says constitutes a counter-offer and thus a rejection of Zoe's original offer (*Hyde* v *Wrench*). This would have the effect of terminating the original offer (*Tinn* v *Hoffmann*) and would thus deny Julia the opportunity of accepting it. As a result, when Julia takes the letter and cheque round to Zoe's house, and slips them under the door, this amounts to the counter-offer, which Zoe is free to accept or reject. However, this interpretation is unlikely to be accepted either because the conversation between Julia and Zoe will be construed in its context – which was informal – and therefore it is unlikely that a court would say a counter-offer has been made.

Yet another interpretation of events is that Zoe has either issued a new offer or she has varied the terms of acceptance of the initial offer ('Oh, forget about that . . . give me a ring sometime'). Either option could apply to Julia, but not to Kathleen since she has received no notification. If there has been a new offer then Julia's acceptance must be by telephone. With instantaneous communications, acceptance must be received: *Entores* v *Miles* 1955, CA. This has not occurred. If Zoe has merely varied the terms of acceptance the issue then is whether or not Julia's note and cheque still constitute a valid acceptance – i.e., does the variation *oust* the initial terms of the offer or merely *supplement* them? If it ousts them then Julia will not have made a valid acceptance, since no one answers her phone call. If, however, Zoe's words in the supermarket are merely intended to supplement the means of accepting the original offer then there is an argument for saying that a binding contract exists between Zoe and Julia. Although the written communication has not arrived by Royal Mail, what Julia has done amounts to the same thing. Therefore Zoe will have to sell the shoes to Julia.

Issue III: Did Kathleen make a valid acceptance?

As a general rule, acceptance takes place when it is brought to the attention of the offeror (here Zoe): *Entores*. However, where the postal rule applies, communication of the acceptance is deemed to have occurred on posting: *Adams v Lindsell*. On this reading, the fact that Kathleen's letter is delayed would be irrelevant: *Household Fire Insurance v Grant* (contract was deemed to be in existence where acceptance, which was posted, never arrived) – a contract would have been formed between Zoe and Kathleen. However, on the facts, it is unclear whether the postal rule actually does apply or whether it has been ousted, as in *Holwell*. Either interpretation is plausible. However it is submitted that by using the words 'post me a written acceptance by Friday morning', Zoe demonstrates an intention to oust the postal rule (as in *Holwell*). If this is correct, then Kathleen's acceptance comes too late.

Issue IV: Can Zoe revoke?

If Julia has accepted Zoe's offer, Zoe cannot revoke it. Zoe will therefore have to go ahead with the agreement or suffer the consequences of her breach of contract. Although an award of damages is the usual contractual remedy, the court may in this instance – owing to the unique value and special interest of the goods in question – make an order for specific performance, requiring the defaulting party (here, Zoe) to carry out her contractual obligations.

Issue V: Will the contract with Julia be void for mistake

Zoe could try to argue that she and Julia have contracted on the basis of a common mistake (that there is some misapprehension about some aspect of the subject-matter of the contract). Shared mistakes as to quality are rarely operative at common law (*Bell* v *Lever Bros* (1931, HL)). It is unlikely therefore that the contract will be declared void. Equity however may deem a contract which has been concluded on the basis of a shared fundamental mistake as to quality voidable (*Solle* v *Butcher* (1950); *Grist* v *Bailey* – where rescission was granted), and the relief, which lies in the court's discretion, may even take the form of refusing to grant specific performance.

Failing a satisfactory remedy under the law on mistake, Zoe's best line of defence is to claim either that what she said about the shoes was an invitation to treat and not an offer, or that she did not intend to create legal relations. Alternatively, she could ask her friends to release her from any legal obligations into which she has entered.

Analysis

What is so special about this answer? On the one hand, there is nothing special about the answer at all. Nothing, that is, that could not be gleaned from a basic textbook outlining the law on offer and acceptance. Certainly there is nothing original about it, neither is everything that could have been teased out of the question addressed e.g., given that the parties were all friends, perhaps the issue of 'intention to create legal relations' should have been given more weight. However, notwithstanding its failings, this answer was awarded a very high mark. Why? Well, there are a number of reasons, and many of them relate back to the suggestions we have already discussed in earlier chapters. First, most of the relevant legal issues have been identified (invitation to treat/offer/acceptance/revocation/intention to create legal relations/mistake). Secondly, the answer is well structured (i.e., the issues are clearly presented) making the material easy to follow and thus easier to mark than answers which are loaded with material but which are structured awkwardly. Thirdly, the law is more than adequately set out and is often accompanied by supporting authority, which is comprehensively yet succinctly applied. Although the analysis is not particularly deep, alternative lines of argument (i.e., different interpretations of the events) are explored. Lastly, the answer argues towards a conclusion, in particular it does not forget to follow the instruction given, which is to advise Zoe. All in all, it represents a significant achievement in terms of recall, organisation and analysis, within the short period of 45 minutes.

In answering the next question a similar type of issues-based structure is presented.

Question

Nicky, an interior decorator, and Simon, a friend who is a builder, are both hit hard by the recession and have time on their hands. Nicky needs a new wall built at the end of her garden. Simon needs some new curtains for his drawing room. Simon tells Nicky that he is happy to build her the wall if she will make up some curtains for him 'in return'. Nicky agrees and Simon starts the wall.

One day when Simon is working, Nicky's neighbour Jo pops in for a coffee. She admires Simon's work, and asks him if he could come round later to fit a new lock to her door. Simon agrees, and later that day fits the lock. Jo is so pleased that she promises to send Simon £50.

The next day Simon receives an offer of immediate temporary employment from a local builder. He tells Nicky that he can only finish the wall if she pays him £250 for the work. Nicky agrees, and Simon turns down the job and finishes the wall.

Now both Nicky and Jo are refusing to pay Simon anything.

Advise Simon.

Answer

For an enforceable contract there must be: (i) an agreement (which can be evidenced by an 'offer' and an 'acceptance'); (ii) intention to create legal relations; and (iii) the contract must be supported by consideration.

Issue I: Is the initial agreement between Simon and Nicky an enforceable contract?

Notwithstanding signs of a bargain (doing something in return for something), the crucial question here is whether there was an intention to create legal relations. Commercial agreements are presumed to create legal relations; however, for social and domestic agreements, the presumption is reversed (*Balfour* v *Balfour* (1919, CA), agreement to pay spouse £30 per week was unenforceable). While this presumption is not easy to rebut, it is nonetheless not impossible: (*Errington* v *Errington* (1952, CA)). See also *Jones* v *Padavatton* (1969, CA), supporting the view that trivial agreements are beyond the scope of the law, but that if agreements have a serious impact on the lives of family members, it is more likely that there was an intention to create legal relations. This approach would appear to be endorsed by the earlier case of *Parker* v *Clark* (1960), where one couple sold their house on the basis that the agreement they had entered into with another couple was legally enforceable.

Applying these principles to the facts, it would appear that there was no intention to create legal relations, since this is a social arrangement within *Balfour* (Nicky (N) and Simon (S) are friends). Although the presumption established in *Balfour* can be rebutted, it is unlikely that this has occurred. The language and context of the arrangement (they have time on their hands and are both hard hit by the recession) points towards an agreement which is not legally binding. This conclusion, however, is by no means certain.

Issue II: Is Jo's promise to pay Simon £50 binding on her?

The requirement of consideration is recognition by the law that contracts should involve some form of bargain or exchange. In addition, the consideration must add to the bargain; it must have moved; and it must not be past.

According to *Pollock*, consideration is 'an act of forbearance of one party, or the promise thereof [being] the price for which the promise of the other is bought'. In other words, did what was provided by one party (be it action, inaction, or a promise thereof), induce the same?

Consideration must be sufficient (i.e., it must have some value in the eyes of the law), but it need not be adequate (*Chappell* v *Nestle* (1960, HL)). The consideration must have moved i.e., a party who has not furnished consideration may not bring an action to enforce a contract (*Dunlop Pneumatic Tyre Co.* v *Selfridge* (1915, HL); *Tweddle* v *Atkinson* (1861)). Where a contract is premised on the basis of an act followed by a promise, the consideration (the promise) will be considered 'past' consideration and will not be enforceable (*Roscorla* v *Thomas* (1842) (involving the sale of a horse); and *Re McArdle* (1951, CA)). However, there are a number of 'exceptions' to the rule that past consideration is not good consideration, the most important of which for present purposes is if there is an understanding that a good or service is to be paid for, albeit that no express agreement has been reached as to the amount payable before the time of performance – the 'requested performance exception' (see *Lampleigh* v *Braithwait* (1615), where the court held that there had been an implied promise to pay for the service rendered). There is also authority to suggest that the court may be more willing to imply a promise to pay when the issue involves a commercial arrangement rather than a domestic one. On this point see *Pao On* v *Lau Yiu Long* (1979, PC), where Lord Scarman laid down three requirements for this exception to operate. First, the act must have been at the promisor's request.

Second, the parties must have understood that the act was to be remunerated either by a payment or the conferment of some benefit. And, third, the payment or benefit must have been legally enforceable had it been promised in advance. (See also: *Re Casey's Patents* (1892); and contrast *Re McArdle* which involved a domestic arrangement – though, in any case, the work had not been requested.)

It might seem therefore that since the act of fitting the lock has already been completed when Jo (J) promises to pay S £50, J's promise is not enforceable (it has not been supported by consideration). However, applying the test laid down in *Pao On*, Simon would argue that (i) the promisor (J) requested that the act be performed, (ii) there was an implicit understanding that remuneration of some sort would be made for fitting the lock, and (iii) had the promise been made in advance, it would have been legally enforceable. In reply J might argue that this was merely a domestic arrangement (falling within *Re McArdle*) and not a commercial arrangement: it was a social agreement over coffee, to which legal relations were not to be attached – it was implicit that S was fitting the lock as a favour. The decision is finely balanced, but given S's state of penury – he was out of work and hard hit by the recession – of which J probably knew, it seems reasonable to assume that this was a commercial arrangement where payment was implicit. Thus J's promise is legally enforceable.

Issue III: Does Simon have a good claim on the payment of £250 by Nicky?

Assuming that the initial agreement between S and N is not enforceable the issue arises whether the subsequent agreement is legally binding. S offers to finish the wall (which on this reading he is under no obligation to do) and in return N promises to pay him £250 to do so. S's consideration is the employment he foregoes/work he does, while N's consideration is her promise to pay S £250 on completion of the wall. There is clearly an intention to create legal relations, since S has turned down the opportunity to take on new work and explicitly says he needs payment (£250). Accordingly, N will be under a binding obligation to pay S the money owed.

If, however, the initial agreement between S and N amounts to a contract, then the issues are much more complex, involving the law applicable to variations of contracts and possibly the law on economic duress.

According to the rule in *Stilk* v *Myrick* (1809), the performance of an existing contractual duty as consideration for a further promise from the party to whom the existing duty was owed is not good consideration. Thus, in that case the promise of extra pay was held to be unenforceable (contrast *Hartley* v *Ponsonby* – where, in more extreme circumstances, the crew was deemed to have gone beyond its duty, and the payment was enforceable). In applying the rule in *Stilk*, it would seem that S has provided no fresh consideration for N's promise to pay him £250. Since S has not gone beyond his duty – the more liberal rule in *Hartley* v *Ponsonby* would not apply. However, the principle in *Stilk* has been severely circumscribed in the Court of Appeal decision of *Williams* v *Roffey* (1990) where it was held that in the event of a further promise being made in a commercial context where both parties intended the further promise made to have legal force, consideration for that promise could be found in the subjective benefit to the person making the promise (promisor) provided the promise was made because of this perceived benefit.

S could argue that, in accordance with the decision in *Williams*, the agreement between him and N was a commercial agreement, that both parties intended the further promises made to have legal force and that N does receive a subjective benefit (getting the wall finished sooner rather than later) and it is this which induces her to make the additional promise. However, there are considerable difficulties in applying the principle in *Williams* to this situation. For example, there is no indication that N gains any factual benefit from the prompt completion of the wall. Moreover, there is a hint of duress on the facts which was not present in *Williams*: S 'tells' N that he cannot complete the wall unless she pays him the extra money. In *Williams*, the plaintiff fully intended to complete. The decision in *Williams* is, therefore, unlikely to prove helpful to S's claim for recovery of the £250.

It is worth noting that promissory estoppel will not help S either. Although he relied to his detriment on a promise, he could only use this as a defence to a claim by N, not as a ground of action to recover the money promised (*Combe* v *Combe* (1951, CA)).

If S is in fact able to rely on *Williams* v *Roffey*, he may still not be able to enforce payment of the £250 on the ground that there has been economic duress (commercial pressure): *Universe Tankships* (1983, HL). It is not entirely clear what N would have to show for economic duress to apply. Certainly the fact that she does not protest about the payment at the time, though not conclusive, would go against her (*The Atlantic Baron* (1979)).

In conclusion, S's best hope is that the initial agreement between him and N is not a contract, but that the later agreement concerning the £250 is. With respect to J, S appears to be on firmer ground since it seems likely that the court will hold that payment for the work was implicit.

Analysis

Again it must be stressed that this method of carving the question up into questions upon which to 'hang' the answer is not the only way to go about answering this or any other problem question – not least because it is always a good idea to demonstrate to the examiner that your mind is sufficiently flexible so as not to be wedded to one particular technique. Nevertheless, this type of approach is extremely effective. The right type of questions are asked and this helps 'set up' the answer, thus leaving the student the task of filling in the boxes by writing out the relevant law and applying it to the facts.

Some points worth considering

(a) Note the different legal issues contained in this contract formation question:

(i) an agreement (which can be evidenced by an 'offer' and an 'acceptance');

(ii) intention to create legal relations; and

(iii) the contract must be supported by consideration.

And note how the examiner leans towards (ii) and (iii) in particular, with different sub-issues being wrapped up inside them, e.g., consideration (past consideration and exceptions). This is extremely common and you must learn to move from the broader picture to those areas where detailed analysis is required.

(b)   An alternative approach which would have been equally good in relation to Issue II is as follows:

> At first sight it might appear that the agreement is not supported by consideration – the act of fitting the lock had already been completed when J promised to pay S £50 – and the rule is that past consideration is not good consideration (see, e.g., *Re McArdle* (1951, CA)). However, there are a number of cases which provide evidence of at least one exception to this rule. In *Re Casey's Patents* (1892), it was held that the promise to pay a manager for services which had been undertaken prior to the promise *was* supported by consideration. As payment was implicit, it was only the amount that needed to be settled. A similar result was reached in the case of *Lampleigh* v *Braithwait*. In the problem before us, the court might find that remuneration was expected, leaving only the amount to be settled. Since it is more likely that a promise to pay will be implied where there is a commercial arrangement rather than a domestic one (see *Pao On* v *Lau Yiu Long* (1979, PC)), it is possible that here S could persuade the court that this was more than a domestic arrangement (his need for work would be one argument in his favour). S would argue in accordance with Lord Scarman's test in *Pao On* that the act (fitting the lock) was done at the promisor's request, (here, J), there was an implicit understanding that remuneration of some sort would be made for fitting the lock (he is already 'at work' when J approaches him), and had the promise been made in advance, it would have been legally enforceable. Although, by no means a foregone conclusion, S's argument is likely to win the day.

This is a slightly more direct approach than the one used in the fuller answer above. One could discuss the reasons why one approach is better than the other, but the point is that both are along the right lines. In both, the issue is identified (consideration, in particular past consideration), the law is set out and it is applied to the facts.

Clearly, how you decide Issue I will influence your answer to Issue III. If the initial agreement between Simon and Nicky is not enforceable, then Issue III involves assessing the relatively straightforward matter of determining whether a contract is formed on the basis of their later negotiations. If, however, there is an initial contract, you must discuss the law relating to variation of contracts. A good answer is one which allows these options to be explored. That means your conclusion on Issue I should merely be provisional and not definitive.

(c)   Although the *Williams* v *Roffey* point in Issue III is difficult, it should not be ignored. The important thing is not to come up with the 'right' answer. Simply make sure that your claims are supported by credible arguments. The aim is to recognise and comment upon difficulties rather than to gloss over them.

2.   EXEMPTION CLAUSES

In an exemption clause question the focus of the answer is not on whether a contract was formed but, having been formed, what the substance of the contract was, i.e., the nature and extent of the rights and obligations which arise under the contract. Unlike the 'bitty' nature of questions on formation, there is a more definite framework available for exemption clause questions around which to weave your material. This should become clear by reading the answer to the following question.

Question

Fry, who was on his way to a book sale, stopped at a fun fair on Bristol Downs, and decided to have a go on Laurie's Bumper Cars. Laurie took his money, and Fry started to drive round. Laurie, however, who was still collecting money, slipped and fell on to the car in front, which stopped suddenly, causing Fry's car to crash into it. After the turmoil has subsided, Fry discovered that a valuable first edition of '*Jeeves and Wooster*', which he had been taking to the sale, had fallen out of his pocket and had been ruined by the bumper car running over it; and that he himself had suffered a whiplash injury. He asked Laurie, 'What are you going to do about it? It's all your fault', but Laurie replied by shrugging his shoulders and pointing to a large sign on the stand saying 'Patrons go on the bumpers at their own risk. No responsibility accepted for any injuries or damage.' These words were repeated on the back of the ticket which Fry had bought.

Advise Fry.

Answer

It would appear that the Laurie (L) is *prima facie* liable for damages for breach of contract, since it could be argued that under s. 13, Sale of Goods and Services Act 1983, there has been a breach of the implied term that the supplier of a service (here, Bumper Cars), acting in the course of a business, must use reasonable care and skill. On this basis, L must show that the exemption clause was legally valid.

The first issue to be decided is whether the exclusion clause was **incorporated** into the contract to use the Bumper Cars. An exclusion clause may only become a term of the contract if reasonable notice of its existence is given before, or at the time when, the contract is made: *Olley* v *Marlborough Court* (1949, CA). There is, however, authority to support the proposition that a printed notice contained on a ticket (as in this problem) may be effective to exclude liability even though it is not actually delivered to the plaintiff until after the moment of agreement between the parties: *Parker* v *SE Railway* (1877, CA). But in *Chapelton* v *Barry UDC* (1940, CA) the court refused to recognise a ticket as a contractual document at all, treating it merely as a receipt for money paid – notice of the clause came too late, since the offer and the acceptance preceded the issuing of the ticket. More recent authorities indicate that reasonable notice must be given and *Parker* may be better interpreted as a case where on the facts reasonable notice was actually given. It is important to note, however, that *Parker* might not be decided in the same way today. In *Thornton* v *Shoe Lane Parking Ltd* (1971, CA), for example, Lord Denning thought that for sufficient notice to be given in a 'ticket' case, it would need to be clearly drawn to the plaintiff's attention (see also: *Interfoto Picture Library* v *Stiletto Visual Programmes* (1988,

CA), where it was held that if the clause is particularly onerous or unusual then it may need to be more clearly drawn to the other party's attention). Whether reasonable steps have been taken to bring the clause to the attention of Fry is a question of fact. Since the decision in *Parker* should be treated with caution, it seems highly unlikely that sufficient notice has been given for the exclusion clause *on the ticket* to be effective.

Whether the sign is incorporated into the contract must also be viewed in the light of the rule mentioned in *Olley* (above). In that case the exclusion clause was read by a hotel guest in the room after booking into the hotel. So reasonable notice had not been given. In the problem before us, however, we are told that L has erected a 'large sign' excluding liability. Thus, in the absence of other facts e.g., that the sign was hidden from view, it can easily be argued that F did have reasonable notice of the sign – and thus of the legal obligations which L was prepared to undertake. On this basis the exclusion clause would be incorporated.

Assuming that the clause does become a term of the contract, L may still not be able to rely on it to escape liability. The issue here is whether the clause covers the type of liability in question (i.e., the loss or damage which has arisen). This is a matter of **construction**. The courts will not imply an exemption greater than that contained in the words used (*Andrews* v *Singer* (1934, CA)). For example, in *Houghton* v *Trafalgar Insurance* (1954) a clause which excluded liability when a car was carrying a *load* in excess of that for which it was constructed, did not exclude liability where the car was carrying an excessive number of *passengers*. Where the words in the clause are ambiguous, the courts construe them *contra proferentem*, that is, against the person seeking to rely on them (*Hollier* v *Rambler Motors*, 1972, CA). Thus, in *White* v *John Warwick* (1953), the Court of Appeal construed an exclusion clause similar to the one in issue in the question as being sufficient to exclude strict contractual liability for personal injury, but not sufficient to exclude liability for injury caused negligently. Very clear words indeed are required to exclude liability in negligence.

On the facts, there is the possibility of strict contractual liability for breach of an implied term that the obligation contracted for (a bumper car ride) would actually be achieved. Laurie will argue that, properly construed, the exclusion clause covers this – an argument which is probably correct. However, the contract is one of providing a 'service' and therefore falls within s. 13, Supply of Goods and Services Act 1982, which implies a term into such a contract that the service will be carried out with reasonable care and skill (i.e., not negligently). The contract has not been so carried out, since Laurie *has* been negligent – it was foreseeable that an accident might happen, if he continued to collect money after the cars had started. Therefore there has been a negligent breach of contract. Applying *White* (above), the exclusion clause will probably not be sufficient to cover liability under s. 13.

Either way there is still a possibility that an exclusion clause may be rendered ineffective by the **Unfair Terms in Consumer Contracts Regulations 1994** or by the **Unfair Contract Terms Act 1977** (UCTA).

The Regulations apply to 'any term in a contract concluded between a *seller or supplier* and a *consumer* where the . . . term has not been individually negotiated'. A 'seller' is a person who sells goods and in making contracts does so for the purposes relating to his business; a 'supplier' is a person who supplies goods or services and in making contracts does so for purposes relating to his business. A 'consumer' means a natural person, who acts for purposes which are outside his business. Prima facie, the contract between F and L falls within the regulations because it is a standard form contract (it has not been individually negotiated), Laurie is offering services (a bumper car ride) in the course of business and Fry has entered into the contract for reasons of pleasure not business.

The effect of the Regulations is to render *unfair terms* inoperative. These are defined as 'any term[s] which, contrary to the requirement of good faith, [cause] a significant imbalance in the parties' rights and obligations arising under the contract to the detriment of the consumer.' Factors taken into account in determining good faith include: the nature of the goods or services; the bargaining position of the parties; whether the seller has dealt fairly and equitably with the consumer; and any other relevant factors. Where there is doubt about the meaning of a written term, the interpretation most favourable to the consumer will prevail. Where the term is held to be 'unfair', it will not be binding on the consumer. The Regulations give an indicative list of terms which are prima facie considered to breach the requirement of good faith, one of which is a term which purports to exclude/limit liability for death or personal injury. Although this is not conclusive, it seems likely that the exclusion clause will be inoperative insofar as F seeks to recover damages for the physical injury (whiplash) that he has sustained (see: sch. 3 para. 1(a)). But even if the Regulations are held not to apply, UCTA s. 2(1) places an absolute prohibition on terms which purport to exclude liability for death or personal injury resulting from negligence in contracts between a supplier acting in the course of a business and a consumer, as in this case.

Damage to F's property (the book) is somewhat more problematic. Under the Regulations, terms which exclude liability other than for death or personal injury are prima facie unfair only if the exclusion is 'inappropriate' (sch. 3 para. 1(b)). In this case, therefore, F may have to rely on UCTA s. 2(2). The effect of the exclusion clause is determined on the basis of whether the term is a fair and reasonable one to have been included in the light of the circumstances known (or which ought to have been) to the parties at the time the contract is made (s. 11). The burden of showing that the clause is 'reasonable' is on the person so claiming (here, L): s. 11(5). It seems reasonable for a user of bumper cars to assume that the owner would not act negligently nor seek to exclude liability for anything which was within the owner's control. F would therefore be entitled to recover damages for his injuries and for the value of the book.

Analysis

(a)   The words in bold (incorporation, construction, Unfair Terms in Consumer Contracts Regulations 1994 and UCTA 1977) represent the key areas on which much of your reading about this topic will have been based. Not surprisingly, it is upon these 'pegs' that the answer has been hung. These issues provide the framework/structure for the answer. Whatever the approach adopted, these issues would have to be confronted in some sort of logical format. Note that the answer starts with a conclusion and then justifies it by reasoned argument.

(b)   Again, the law is set out in relation to each issue and then it is applied. For example:

[Issue]   The first issue to be decided is whether the exclusion clause
                 contained in the ticket or the sign was **incorporated** into the
                 contract to use the Bumper Cars.

[Rule]   An exclusion clause may only become a term of the contract if
                 reasonable notice of its existence is given before, or at the time
                 when, the contract is made: *Olley* v *Marlborough Court* (1949,
                 CA). There is, however, authority to support the proposition that a
                 printed notice contained on a ticket (as in this problem) may be
                 effective to exclude liability even though it is not actually delivered
                 to the plaintiff until after the moment of agreement between the
                 parties: *Parker* v *SE Railway* (1877, CA). But in *Chapelton* v *Barry
                 UDC* (1940, CA) the court refused to recognise a ticket as a
                 contractual document at all, treating it merely as a receipt for
                 money paid – notice of the clause came too late, since the offer and
                 the acceptance preceded the issuing of the ticket. More recent
                 authorities indicate that reasonable notice must be given and *Parker*
                 may be better interpreted as a case where on the facts reasonable
                 notice was actually given. It is important to note, however, that
                 Parker might not be decided in the same way today. In *Thornton* v
                 Shoe Lane Parking Ltd (1971, CA), for example, Lord Denning
                 thought that for sufficient notice to be given in a 'ticket' case, it
                 would need to be clearly drawn to the plaintiff's attention (see also:
                 Interfoto Picture Library v *Stiletto Visual Programmes* (1988, CA),
                 where it was held that if the clause is particularly onerous or
                 unusual then it may need to be more clearly drawn to the other
                 party's attention).

[Application and Whether reasonable steps have been taken to bring the clause to the
Conclusion]   attention of F is a question of fact. Since the decision in *Parker*
                 should be treated with caution it seems highly unlikely that
                 sufficient notice has been given for the exclusion clause *on the
                 ticket* to be effective. Whether the sign is incorporated into the
                 contract must also be viewed in the light of the rule mentioned in
                 Olley (above). In that case the exclusion clause was read by a hotel
                 guest in the room after booking into the hotel. So reasonable notice
                 had not been given. In the problem before us, however, we are told
                 that L has erected a 'large sign' excluding liability. Thus, in the
                 absence of other facts e.g., that the sign was hidden from view, it
                 can easily be argued that F did have reasonable notice of the sign
                 – and thus of the legal obligations which Laurie was prepared to
                 undertake. On this basis the exclusion clause would be incorpor-
                 ated.

(c)   Note that the issue of the ticket as a exclusion clause is considered first
and then rejected before going on to consider the legal significance of the sign
(which is deemed to be incorporated). If you were to do it the other way round,
you would incorporate the sign, thus making the issue of whether the ticket is
an exclusion clause redundant. Remember, you are an examinee and the aim is

to display as much *relevant* knowledge to the examiner as possible, even if this may seem highly artificial at times.

(d)   The question raises the difficult problem of the relationship between the Unfair Terms in Consumer Contracts Regulations 1994 and UCTA 1977, but just because this is unclear does not mean that it can be legitimately avoided. In discussing the Regulations most of the relevant law is set out first (the definition of the terms) and then applied. During the 'application' stage, an additional legal rule is introduced, namely: 'The Regulations give an indicative list of terms which are prima facie considered to breach the requirement of good faith, one of which is a term that purports to exclude/limit liability for death or personal injury. Keeping material like this 'in reserve' is a perfectly sensible approach to use and is illustrative of the fact that any approach adopted must be sufficiently flexible to accommodate slightly different ways of analysing problems. By contrast to the approach used in discussing the Regulations, the material in relation to UCTA 1977 is handled more sparingly. The law is not set out first and then applied; rather, fact and law are intertwined.

3.   MISREPRESENTATION AND (SOME) MISTAKE

The existence of 'vitiating factors', such as misrepresentation and mistake, can affect the validity of a contract that parties have entered into. The answers to the remaining questions in this chapter illustrate this issue well. Note how the 'scheme' presented below can be used as a way of helping you to *think* about, and subsequently structure, your answer:

(i)   Are the statements representations or terms?

(ii)   If they are representations, are they actionable (i.e., are they misrepresentations which induce the other party to enter into the contract)?

(iii) If they are misrepresentations, of what type are they (i.e., fraudulent, negligent, or wholly innocent)?

(iv)   What remedies are available?

Question

(a)   Gerard, who has won a large sum of money, goes to Rod, who owns an exclusive art gallery in London. Gerard points at a painting and says 'Tell me about this one. How much are you asking?' Rod, who knows that the painting is by a minor English artist, says, 'I cannot be absolutely certain, but it is my opinion that it is a Renoir. I'll sell it to you for £100,000.' Gerard buys the painting, which is actually worth only £5,000.

AND

(b)   David, a wealthy art collector, visits Rod and they enthuse together about a painting hanging in the gallery. 'It's a beautiful example of Botticelli's work,' says

Rod. David, who normally only collects English landscapes, buys the painting for £100,000 as a present for his girlfriend, and arranges to take the painting away.

Unfortunately the painting is damaged in transit, and when David takes it to a restorer, he is told that the painting is actually by a pupil of Botticelli, and would really be worth only £20,000, after restoration, which would cost £6,000. In fact there had recently been an article about the painting in an art journal, to which both David and Rod subscribe, reattributing the work.

What remedies, if any, do Gerard and David have against Rod?

Answer

(a) Gerard and Rod

Gerard (G) will want to sue Rod (R) for damages and/or he may want to rescind the contract (i.e., have it set aside). Applying an objective test of the parties intentions, the statement made by R is probably a representation rather than a term – it was certainly not dogmatic (*Schawel* v *Reade*, 1913, HL). The issue then arises as to whether the representation is actionable – whether R made a *false statement of fact*, which, whilst not a term of the contract, *induced* G to enter the contract. A 'mere puff' (*Carlill* v *Carbolic Smoke Ball*, 1893, CA) will not amount to a misrepresentation; neither will a statement of opinion (*Bisset* v *Wilkinson*, 1927, PC). However, where the opinion offered is dishonest, the false statement can amount to a misrepresentation (*Smith* v *Land & House Property Corp* (1884)). Since R 'knows' that the painting is not a Renior, but says that it is, he has, 'knowingly', made a 'false statement of fact' (the fact of whether or not that is his honest opinion). In this respect, the qualification 'I cannot be absolutely certain . . .', when taken in its context, is irrelevant.

The next issue to consider is whether the false statement of fact induces G to enter into the contract. Usually, this means that G must show that the statement was material (i.e., that it would cause a reasonable person, considering entering into the contract, to decide positively in favour of doing so). However, where there is fraud (as here) this requirement is dispensed with (*Smith* v *Kay*, (1859)). It must be shown that G relied on R's statement (contrast *Attwood* v *Small* (1838), where P relied on an independent expert's advice and so was denied a remedy for misrepresentation). Nonetheless, the fact that G was given the opportunity to test its accuracy is irrelevant (*Redgrave* v *Hurd* (1881, CA)), as is the fact that R's misrepresentation may not be the only reason why G entered into the contract: *Edgington* v *Fitzmaurice* (1885).

The next issue is to decide what type of misrepresentation has been made: fraudulent, negligent, or innocent. This is important from the point of view of the remedies granted by the courts. On the facts of the problem, the misrepresentation is fraudulent, since R has knowingly made a false statement (*Derry* v *Peek* (1889, HL)). Damages are available and are calculated on tortious (out-of-pocket) principles, rather than contractual (loss-of-bargain) principles (fraudulent misrepresentation is the tort of deceit).

* * *

In addition to damages, a fraudulent misrepresentation renders the contract voidable. In other words, G could get an order for rescission. Where the contract is rescinded, the object is to put the parties back in the position they would have been in had the contract never been made. However, certain 'bars' to rescission exist (i.e., in certain circumstances P may lose his right to rescind). The most important 'bar' from G's point of view is where P is deemed to have *affirmed* the contract. Lapse of time may be evidence of affirmation: *Leaf* v *International Galleries* (1950, CA).

* * *

(b) David and Rod

Applying the test set out in part (a), it would appear that R's statement, 'It's a beautiful example of Botticelli's work' is, again, a false statement of fact. However it is less certain whether there has been an inducement. If David (D) buys the painting irrespective of whether it is by Botticelli, but simply because he knows his girlfriend will like it, then no inducement will have occurred, since he has not relied on R's statement (*Attwood* v *Small*). On the other hand, if his girlfriend likes only Botticelli, this will be strong evidence that R's statement was a material factor in inducing D to enter into the contract. Alternatively, even if his girlfriend does like only Botticelli it could be inferred that since D subscribes to the art journal he relies only on his own judgment and not R's. However, his failure to inform R of this matter (i.e., to put him right) is surely significant, since it implies that he was not aware of the reattribution (though, equally, this may raise an issue of contributory negligence on D's part).

Assuming that there has been an inducement, it is again necessary to classify the misrepresentation and so determine the remedies available. In this instance there is no indication of the type of misrepresentation made. If it is fraudulent, the above mentioned rules in part (a) will apply. If the misrepresentation is negligent (i.e., it is a statement that no reasonable man would have made), then remedies are available at common law and under statute. At common law, damages are available in certain circumstances for the tort of negligent misstatement (*Hedley Byrne*, 1964, HL). More relevant to the present problem, however, is s. 2(1) of the Misrepresentation Act 1967 which has significant advantages over a claim at common law. This section assumes that all non-fraudulent statements are negligent and puts the burden on the maker of the statement to disprove negligence. However, the alleged misrepresentor will not have to pay damages if (i) he proves that he had reasonable grounds to believe *and* (ii) he did believe up to the time the contract was made that the facts represented were true. R – as the alleged misrepresentor – will argue that he had not read the journal and thus reasonably believed that what he was saying was true and that this is what he did believe until after the contract was formed. Notwithstanding this, D is in a very strong position, since the burden of proof is on Rod. It would therefore seem likely that D would be entitled to damages. These are more favourable under the Misrepresentation Act (*Royscot* v *Rogerson,* 1991, CA, calculated on the same basis as fraudulent misrepresentation) than at common law. Again, D will be entitled to rescind the contract, subject to any bars.

It is also possible that the misrepresentation was innocent (i.e., a statement made by a person who *has* reasonable grounds for believing in its truth, but which is nonetheless false). If a misrepresentation is wholly innocent then the victim is only entitled to rescission (and an indemnity, see below). However, according to s. 2(2), Misrepresentation Act 1967 the court has a discretion, where the other party would be entitled to rescind, to award damages instead of rescission – and perhaps even where the misrepresentation in question is not sufficient to ground a right of rescission: *William Sindall* v *Cambridgeshire CC* (1994, CA). Where rescission is available, it is generally possible to recover an indemnity as well. An indemnity provides compensation for expenditure incurred as a result of obligations which have been created by the contract into which the representee has been induced to enter (see: *Whittington* v *Seale-Hayne* (1900)).

Although the painting has been damaged in transit, and it might seem that this creates a bar to rescission, it is not necessary for there to be exact restoration; the remedy is still available if substantial restoration is possible. Although the exact nature of the damage done is not specified, it would seem that substantial restoration is possible and that the court could therefore use its discretion to award damages in lieu of rescission. However in the light of the Court of Appeal's decision in *William Sindall* it may no longer be necessary for rescission to be available.

D could also allege that the contract is void for mistake (here, common mistake – the parties, though in apparent agreement, have contracted on the same false assumption). Although it is possible that a contract will make provision for allocation of risk in the event of some misunderstanding (*Clark* v *Lindsay*, 1993), there is no evidence to suppose that this rule is relevant. The common law takes a *narrow* view of the type of mistake which will render a contract void (and thus for it to be deemed never to have existed): it must be shown that there was a shared fundamental mistake as to the *existence* of the subject-matter of the contract (*Galloway* v *Galloway; Strickland* v *Turner*; and *Bell* v *Lever* (1931, HL)). However three of their Lordships in *Bell* did say that a sufficiently fundamental mistake as to *quality, might* render the contract void at common law. This was especially so where the mistake rendered the thing 'essentially different' from that which it was believed to be. Nevertheless, their Lordships, in applying this test, took such a restrictive view that it has been doubted whether any mistake as to quality can ever be sufficiently fundamental at common law. On this reading of *Bell*, it would seem highly unlikely that the mistake as to quality in the problem (mistaking the pupil for the master) would be legally operative (see also: *Leaf*, a case on similar facts to the problem). However, it has been suggested that *Bell* is a 'quite exceptional case' (*Associated Japanese Bank* v *Credit Nord* (1988) *per* Steyn J) and there are those who would say that a better (though not generally accepted) view is that such a mistake should be regarded as sufficiently fundamental to render the contract void (*Treitel*).

Failing this, equitable remedies may be available. The court in exercising its *equitable jurisdiction* can, where there is a common mistake as to *quality*, say that it is *voidable* in equity, even though the agreement is valid at common law. The relief, which lies in the court's discretion, may take the form of refusing to grant specific performance (that is, refusing to force the parties to go ahead with the contract). Alternatively, the court may actually grant specific performance or allow rescission, though it is not certain which mistakes are sufficient to render a contract capable of being rescinded in equity. An example of where a contract has been set aside is *Solle* v *Butcher* (1950, CA), which involved a mistake of quality (which at common law is irrelevant). The drawback to this approach, however, is that only equitable remedies are available, which are subject to the same bars as those applicable to misrepresentation.

Analysis

(a)   The first point to note relates to the identification of the legal issues. As suggested earlier, the legal significance of the various statements made are analysed in relation to the relevant legal rules. For example, in part (a), the statement 'I cannot be absolutely certain, but it is my opinion that it is a Renoir' is analysed in terms of its legal significance: is it a term or merely a representation; and, if it is the latter, is it actionable?

(b) The second point relates to structure: you will see that the organising framework revolves around pairing up the parties. Within this framework, there has been adopted in part (a) a variation of the IRAC method. If you were to adopt this modified version of IRAC you would need to:

(i)   identify the relevant remedies appropriate to the parties (here, damages and rescission);

(ii)   state the law relating to the remedy sought – the cause of action (the law on misrepresentation); and

(iii)   apply the law to the facts, stating what further facts (if any) you would need to provide more concrete advice.

This approach is not, however, without its problems. Most significantly, it requires a student to make at the outset an accurate assessment of the relevant remedies that are available and the steps that must be covered to secure those remedies. This may be asking a lot of a student, especially in the 'heat' of an exam. However, students usually decide early on in the assessment of the answer where the balance of liability lies, and thus do have a rough idea of where the answer will end up. This ability to survey the terrain quickly and find out the 'lie of the land', so to speak, is invaluable in determining the relevant remedies. Of course, if you do not feel confident about conducting a survey of this nature, you could always leave a couple of lines blank, work through the steps necessary to obtain the remedy and then, when you have explained that the remedy is available, go back to the beginning and say 'Gerard will be able to sue Rod for damages, for misrepresentation, and/or will be able to rescind the contract, i.e., have it set aside', or something along these lines.

(c) The third point to note relates to the application of the relevant law to the facts. In both parts (a) and (b), the law on misrepresentation is set out in stages and applied. For example: (i) the false statement; (ii) the inducement; (iii) the remedies; and so on. Setting out the law in stages like this helps you to formulate your answer, as well as helping the examiner follow what you are doing and where you are going. In part (b), although there is clearly a false statement, it is a lot less certain whether an inducement has occurred. But to prevent an 'exit' from the question too early the conclusion is made that an inducement does exist. For example:

However it is less certain whether there has been an inducement. If D buys the painting irrespective of whether it is by Botticelli, but simply because he knows his girlfriend will like it, then no inducement will have occurred, since he has not relied on R's statement (*Attwood* v *Small*). On the other hand, if his girlfriend likes only Botticelli, this will be strong evidence that R's statement was a material factor in inducing D to enter into the contract. Alternatively, even if his girlfriend does like only Botticelli it could be inferred that since D subscribes to the art journal he relies only on his own judgment and not R's. However, his failure to inform R of this matter (i.e., to put him right) is surely significant, since it implies that he was not aware of the reattribution (though, equally, this may raise an issue of contributory negligence on D's part).

Assuming that there has been an inducement . . .

This sort of approach is permissible only if you have offered arguments for both points of view and there are at least some plausible arguments in favour of your conclusion, albeit that the matter is a finely balanced one.

(d) It will no doubt have struck you that the answer is very long; and if – as in this answer – you have a lot of ground to cover, you may need to modify the way in which you set out the law and apply it to the facts. This will mean that instead of explaining the law and then applying it to the facts, you have to interweave law and fact more adroitly. This sort of approach is more sophisticated, since it is much less formulaic. The down side, however, is that it is harder to teach to students, since the processes involved are altogether more subtle and if not done properly could result in the loss of marks. A good example of the approach in action is as follows:

Given that R has knowingly made a false statement of fact, the misrepresentation is fraudulent (*Derry* v *Peek* (1889, HL)) and damages are payable on the basis of tortious (out-of-pocket) principles.

Yet again:

Since there is an argument that a bar to rescission exists (the painting has been 'damaged in transit' – so restoration is no longer possible) it might seem that the court will be unable to exercise its discretion to award damages in lieu of rescission in accordance with s. 2(2), Misrepresentation Act 1967. However, in the light of the Court of Appeal's decision in *William Sindall* v *Cambridgeshire CC* (1994), it may no longer be necessary for rescission to be available before this remedy can be granted.

(e) Note also that in the final part of (b) – dealing with mistake – a 'double-decker' approach has been used, i.e., the mistake is first considered at common law (the first layer) and, if no relief is forthcoming, the position of the mistake in equity is reviewed (the second layer).

4. MISTAKE AND (SOME) MISREPRESENTATION

Question

Guy is an amateur breeder of Caucasian Elk hounds. He puts an advertisement in the *Dog Lovers' Weekly* saying: 'Elk hound called Lionheart for sale, £500. Must go to a good home, therefore offer open only to members of the Elk Hound Appreciation Society.' Marian, who resembles Lady Sheriff, the president of the Society, goes to see the dog, and then tells Guy that she has fallen in love with Lionheart and is desperate to take him home immediately. When she offers Guy a cheque, Guy asks: 'Please may I have some other identification, Lady Sheriff?' Marian suggest that he telephones the Appreciation Society, and gives him a number which he duly rings. Robin (a close friend of Marian) answers the phone and confirms that the person with whom Guy is dealing is the president of the Society. Guy, who is now satisfied that Marian is who she claims to be, allows her to take Lionheart home.

The cheque is subsequently dishonoured, and Guy discovers that Marian has given the dog to Robin, who runs an export agency and has sent Lionheart to Iceland to pull sledges. Marian has disappeared.

Advise Guy.

Answer

It may be possible for Guy (G) to have the contract with Marian (M) set aside for mistake. If the contract is deemed void for mistake, it will be unenforceable by either party, title to the property in question will be unable to pass, and any money paid out will be recoverable. It is irrelevant that a long time has elapsed (as in *Leaf*), or that innocent third parties are in charge of the subject-matter of the contract (compare the position with misrepresentation) – third parties will have to return the goods to the 'true owner' because the contract is deemed never to have existed.

Given the dire consequences of holding a contract to be void, very few mistakes are considered to be 'legally operative'. The type of mistake at issue here is a unilateral mistake i.e., a situation where one party is mistaken concerning the contract and the other party is aware of the mistake. Unilateral mistakes often occur in relation to cases of mistaken identity (as in the facts of the problem). The rule is that where the unilateral mistake relates to the *identity* of the other contracting party the mistake will be operative (*Cundy* v *Lindsay* (1876, HL)), but where the mistake merely relates to an *attribute* of the person (e.g., the creditworthiness of the other party) the mistake will not render the contract void (*Kings Norton* v *Edridge* (1897, CA)). Instead, the contract would merely be voidable on the basis of fraud. It could be argued that this is a distinction without a difference (*per* Lord Denning MR in *Lewis* v *Avery* (i.e., people are identified by reference to their attributes); certainly it is a difficult distinction to draw, especially when the parties deal, not by letter, but face-to-face (*Phillips* v *Brooks* (1919, CA); *Ingram* v *Little* (1960, CA); and *Lewis* v *Averay* (1971, CA)). The normal presumption when dealing face-to-face is that there is an intention to deal with the person who is physically present (*per* Pearce LJ in *Ingram* v *Little*). However, this presumption is capable of being rebutted where '[the] identity [of the other party is] of vital importance' (*per* Pearce LJ, *Ingram* v *Little*).

Applying these principles to the facts, a good argument can be made that G does not intend to deal with the person in front of him, but with the President of the Society. He is not merely interested in her credit-worthiness (a lack of which could be considered a risk which all business people must take). The dictum of Pearce LJ in *Ingram* v *Little* quoted above, is directly in point. G is not interested in the money, but in finding an appropriate owner for his dog – someone who will offer the dog a good home and who is a member of the Elk Hound Appreciation Society. Alternatively, it may be that at the time of the sale his only concern was with M's creditworthiness – in which case the contract would not be void for mistake, but merely *voidable* for misrepresentation **[discuss misrepresentation using the principles outlined earlier: did M make a false statement of fact which . . . ?]**.

Assuming that there is a fraudulent misrepresentation, G is entitled to damages and rescission. However, since M has disappeared, G will be unable to sue for damages (unless he is aware of her assets upon which he could make a claim). At first blush, therefore, it would seem that rescission offers a more promising remedy. Although a third party *acting in good faith* who has acquired the goods *for value* before the contract has been rescinded is protected by the law, Robin (R) could not claim this protection (s. 23, Sale of Goods Act 1979). He does not pay for the dog (M gives the dog to him). Also, he is not in good faith. It may be inferred from the facts that R colluded with M in order to dupe G into believing that she was Lady Sheriff (R replied to the phonecall requesting clarification of her status). In theory, therefore, R will have to return the dog to G.

The dog, of course, is in Iceland, and the issue arises whether R has sold the dog on to another party acting in good faith and for value. What exactly has happened is unclear from the facts – we are told merely that R runs an export agency and has 'sent' the dog to Iceland. This would imply that no sale has taken place. However, even if G demonstates this and the fact that R was in bad faith, problems still remain. Since the dog is now in Iceland and may no longer be capable of being traced it could be that restoration is no longer possible (i.e., a bar to rescission exists).

R's apparently false statement is of no significance other than to establish his bad faith.

Analysis

Again, focus attention on the approach used. The student has located the area of contract: mistake (with some misrepresentation). Note the significance of a legally operative mistake (severe consequences). Categorise the mistake (unilateral). Give a definition. Offer an example. Set out the relevant law (i.e., when is a mistake legally operative?). Apply the law to the facts. If the mistake is not legally operative, are there other remedies? Misrepresentation? Remedies? Rescission? Bars?

In relation to applying the law to the facts of the problem, note in particular the section where the law on unilateral mistakes is set out and then applied. Having outlined the appropriate law, the answer continues:

Applying these principles to the facts, a good argument can be made that G was interested in the identity of the person with whom he contracted and not merely her creditworthiness, since he is not only interested in the money but in finding an appropriate owner for his dog – someone who will offer the dog a 'good home' and who is a member of the Elk Hound Appreciation Society. Alternatively, it may be that at the time of the sale his only concern was with M's creditworthiness – in which case the contract would not be void for mistake, but merely *voidable* for misrepresentation.

The above approach may be contrasted with the following:

> If the court determines that Guy's mistake relates to identity then the contract may be deemed void; but if it is deemed merely to relate to attributes (e.g. creditworthiness) then it will not be void.

This is no more than a statement of the problem. You must try, as far as the question allows, to use the facts to advance an argument.

This is a short answer, and short answers rarely score well. But there is not much else in the question and most of what is there has been covered. In this sort of situation, it is probably best to delve into the cases a little more. In fact there could have been a more detailed discussion of *Phillips* v *Brooks, Ingram* v *Little,* and *Lewis* v *Averay.*

Chapter 4

Public Law

On first impression it might seem that public law as a subject is unsuited to the application of a common problem-solving approach. After all, the wide-ranging nature of public law – spanning criminal and civil liability and often, and more importantly, touching on political sanctions – suggests that it is very different from the other subjects we have so far considered. In the absence of a formal written British Constitution, students are often struck by the flexibility of the subject-matter and, in particular, by the influence of politics in the area of constitutional law (e.g., the Queen's theoretical power to choose her ministers and the political practice – convention – that the candidates for ministerial office are nominated by the Prime Minister). However, some of the difficulties and significant differences that do exist may be mitigated by the fact that examiners recognise that certain areas of public law are more conducive to being examined in problem form than others. For example, it is unusual (though possible) to see a problem question on areas such as the sources of the British Constitution, the rule of law, or constitutional conventions. The conceptual nature of these topics means that they tend to appear in examinations as essay questions (see chapter 5 on answering essay questions). By way of contrast, other areas of public law (e.g., police powers, public order, public interest immunity, European Community law and judicial review) are often examined in problem form. Notwithstanding the fact that significant differences do still remain, they are not such that they invalidate the methods employed in earlier sections of this book, in terms of identifying issues and extracting the relevant rules and principles of law, which are then applied to facts in order to reach credible conclusions.

In this chapter, we shall look at problem questions from each of the three parts into which most public law courses are divided: (1) general principles of constitutional law; (2) rights and liberties of the individual; and (3) administrative law – your course may, however, have different characteristics and you should pay close attention to them. On general principles of constitutional law, we shall look at two questions: one on Parliamentary supremacy, European Community law, and the European Convention on Human Rights; and the other on judicial accountability. For the civil liberties section, a police powers and public order question will covered. Lastly, administrative law will be illustrated by a problem question on judicial review. In addition to employing the more general techniques already outlined and adopted in earlier chapters, special attention is again paid to 'micro' structures, which will be of help in answering questions in the above specified areas.

1. CONSTITUTIONAL LAW

Question

Ral is a British citizen. As a practicing Phob (a devout religious minority), Ral is required by religious law to cover his head at all times in public, by wearing a large soft woollen hat, a 'kap'. Ral works in the construction trade on a building site, where all workers are legally required to wear 'hard hats' (safety helmets). However, for the last decade, as a result of the Religious Exemption Act 1985 (fictitious), Ral and other Phob workers have been specifically excluded from this requirement and have been allowed to wear their kaps.

One morning Ral is called into the office of Bob, the site manager. Bob explains that the company has been forced to introduce a new policy – that to comply with a recently published EC Council Regulation (No. 400/95), all workers in the construction trade must now wear 'hard hats'. Bob explains that unless Ral removes his kap and replaces it with a company issued 'hard hat', his monthly contract of employment will not be renewed.

Ral's 17-year-old daughter, Fay, attends a state school. Her Local Education Authority has introduced a policy that any pupil who comes to school wearing anything other than the regulation school uniform (which excludes the wearing of anything on one's head) will immediately be sent home. Since Fay has refused to remove her kap, she has been denied access to the school for the last 26 weeks. She is worried that this will damage her chances of going to university to study medicine. A private tutor, who has been hired to teach Fay at home for one day a week, considers that Fay has the ability to study medicine, but is concerned that she has fallen well behind other students of her age who enjoy the benefits of a full-time education. Fay discovers from a friend who is a law student that EC Directive 125/96 provides that all Phoban students should be permitted to keep their heads covered and wear their kaps in schools. This Directive had a time limit of 1 July 1996 for implementation, but has not as yet been implemented by the UK.

Ignoring any issues relating to racial discrimination, employment law, or parental choice, advise Ral and Fay.

Answer

(a) Ral

(i) Can Ral rely on the 1985 Act of Parliament? In this question there is a conflict between domestic legislation (the Religious Exemption Act 1985) and a piece of

Community legislation (Regulation No. 400/95). Notwithstanding the fact that British courts have traditionally respected the legislative supremacy of Parliament (*Cheney* v *Conn* (1968)), Parliament chose to pass the European Communities Act (ECA) 1972, giving the force of law to those provisions of Community law which are directly effective (s. 2(1) and (4)).

In addressing the issue of whether the Act of Parliament may take precedence over an EC Regulation, the position of the European Court of Justice (ECJ) is clear: Community law prevails over subsequent incompatible national law (*Internationale Handelsgesellschaft:* 11/70 (1970) ECJ). Were this not so, the attainment of Community objectives would be jeopardised (*Costa* v *ENEL*). Thus Community law has created a 'new order of international law' by which states have limited their sovereign rights in certain areas (*Van Gend en Loos* (1963, ECJ)). Since the ECJ has instructed national courts that they must 'disapply' national law which is in conflict with EC law, it is indisputable that at Community level, EC law is supreme.

Unfortunately for Ral (R), British law has increasingly adopted the same approach. Despite the fact that the UK courts have long held that an Act of Parliament is not invalid if it conflicts with a treaty to which the UK is a signatory (*Cheney* v *Conn*), the Treaty of Rome and the other treaties establishing the EC, are not ordinary treaties – they have been incorporated into British law in the form of the ECA 1972. The primacy of Community law was accepted by the House of Lords in *R* v *Secretary of State for Transport, ex parte Factortame* (1990), where a group of Spanish fishermen complained that certain provisions of the Merchant Shipping Act 1988 prevented them from registering their boats in the UK. They sought an interim injunction, claiming that parts of the 1988 Act were incompatible with EC law prohibiting discrimination against other Community nationals. Following a preliminary ruling from the ECJ, the House of Lords ruled that it was the duty of a British court to override a rule of national law which is in direct conflict with a directly enforceable rule of Community law.

Since regulations are 'directly applicable' and do not require member states to take any action for them to become part of their national law (EC Treaty, Art. 189), Regulation No. 400/95 will take precedence over the Act in this scenario (*Factortame*). Subsequent cases endorse the *Factortame* decision (*McKecknie* v *UBM* (1991)), so R has little chance of relying on the 1985 Act of Parliament.

(ii)   Can Ral challenge the regulation?   R may also seek judicial review by the ECJ of the regulation (EC Treaty, Art. 173). There are two hurdles in the way of an individual such as R seeking to challenge a piece of Community legislation. First, an individual must comply with certain procedural requirements (i.e., *locus standi* and a two-month time limit). Secondly, the individual must satisfy at least one of the substantive grounds for a legal challenge. The test for *locus standi* is one of individual concern – that the individual seeking judicial review is affected by reason of certain attributes which are peculiar to him or her (*Plaumann* v *Commission* (1963, ECJ)). R can argue that as a Phob, for whom the wearing of the kap is a compulsory religious requirement, the regulation is of direct concern to him. This test is quite rigid, so to avoid the *locus standi* hurdle, R may choose to sue in the national courts for unfair dismissal and hope that the case is referred to the ECJ under Art. 177 of the EC Treaty. Even if R satisfies the *locus standi* requirement and complies with the time limit, he will have difficulty challenging the regulation on substantive grounds. The four

grounds for such a challenge are that the Community body (i) lacked competence; (ii) failed to comply with an essential procedural requirement; (iii) infringed the EC Treaty or any rule of law relating to its application; or (iv) misused its power (EC Treaty, Art. 173). If R can show that any of these are present, the ECJ would declare the regulation void (EC Treaty, Art. 174). R's strongest argument will be on the basis of (iii), given the regulation's impact on the 'fundamental rights' of Phobs (*Nold* v *Commission* (1974)). Whilst fundamental rights have been recognised as 'general principles of Community Law' (Maastricht Treaty 1992, Art. F(2)), R should remember that no Community measure has as yet been struck down on the ground of non-observance of fundamental human rights.

(iii)   Ral's remedies under the ECHR   R's final remedy is the European Convention on Human Rights (ECHR). Since it has not been incorporated into British law (*R* v *Home Secretary for the Home Department, ex parte Brind* (1991, HL)), he will have to apply to the European Commission on Human Rights to invoke this international human rights treaty. R should be aware of two issues: (a) the ECHR's procedural requirements and (b) the substantive grounds for a successful application.

(a)   The European Commission accepts petitions from individuals complaining that they are victims of a violation of the ECHR (Art. 25). If R submits an individual petition, the European Commission must first decide whether it is admissible. The Commission will check that R has exhausted all available domestic remedies and that the final petition is brought within six months of the final decision in the British courts (Art. 26). Assuming that the Commission feels that there is merit in R's case, it will draw up a report and refer the case to the European Court of Human Rights. A decision of the European Court is final (i.e., there are no appeals), and should R be successful he could be awarded compensation by the Court (Art. 50).

(b)   R is likely to invoke Art. 9(1) (freedom of religion), which guarantees the right to manifest one's religion or belief 'in worship, teaching, practice or observance'. R is likely to argue that by wearing his kap, he is manifesting a religious belief. However, this general freedom is subject to qualification under Art. 9(2). Curbs may be placed on the right to manifest one's religion, where the restriction satisfies the following three criteria:

(i)   it is 'prescribed by law' (Reg. No. 400/95);

(ii)   it is necessary in a democratic society (the European Court defined this to mean that there is a 'pressing social need' for the restriction (*Dudgeon* v *UK* (1981)); and

(iii)   it is justified as necessary to protect 'public health'.

In an earlier case (*X* v *UK No. 7992/77*) the European Commission rejected an application submitted by a Sikh motor cyclist, who claimed that road traffic legislation compelling him to wear a crash helmet and not his turban while riding his motorcycle, was a violation of Art.9. The European Commission held that the compulsory wearing of crash helmets was a necessary safety measure for motor cyclists, and that any interference with freedom of religion was justified as necessary for the protection of health (Art. 9(2)). Whilst the European Commission is not strictly bound by its previous decisions, they are of considerable persuasive value. Thus it is unlikely that

R would succeed in any petition under Art. 9. He might invoke Art. 10, freedom of expression, but it is uncertain whether wearing a kap would constitute 'expression' for the purposes of this article. And even if it did, the same kinds of limits can be placed on the freedom of expression on the ground of public safety as those earlier mentioned (Art. 10(2)). Lastly, the public safety point is also relevant if R was to claim that there is discrimination (Art. 14), because the European Court has held that different treatment is acceptable when it has an objective and reasonable justification (*Belgian Linguistics case* (1967)). Thus the ECHR is of little assistance to R.

It would seem that since legal redress is not likely, R should seek political redress, by petitioning the European and Westminster Parliaments. Ultimately his success may depend on mobilising the Phobs as a group, generating media publicity and winning public support for his cause.

(b) Fay

The issue here is whether Fay (F) may rely on the directive so that she can keep her head covered in school. The EC Treaty provides that a directive is binding as to the result to be achieved on each member state, although the national authorities retain the power to decide the choice and method of its implementation (EC Treaty, Art. 189). The date of a directive's entry into force is decisive. Where the time limit for its implementation has passed, the directive may have *direct effect* (*Ratti* (1979, ECJ)). This is the principle that Community law can create rights and obligations which may be enforced in the national courts.

In view of this, F will seek to rely on Directive 125/96 in the UK courts. For it to be directly effective, she will have to show that it is sufficiently clear, precise and unconditional, so that the UK has no discretion in its implementation (*Van Duyn* v *Home Office* (1974, ECJ)). It is significant here that the directive's time limit for implementation has passed – this is important for F, since a directive cannot be directly effective before its time limit has expired (*Ratti*). Thus it seems that F will be able to invoke Directive 125/96 'vertically' against the UK.

F could argue that since the UK was under an obligation to implement the Directive (EC Treaty, Art. 5), it is under a duty to compensate her for loss suffered as a result of its failure to do so. In this respect, the decision by the ECJ in *Francovich* v *Italy* (1990, ECJ) may be relevant. There the Court held that a member state may be required to compensate individuals for a failure to implement a directive if three conditions are shown to have been satisfied. These are that:

(i)   the directive involved rights conferred on individuals;
(ii)   those rights could be identified from the directive's provisions; and
(iii)   that there was a causal link between the state's failure and the damage suffered by the persons affected.

Assuming that the directive is phrased to satisfy the first two criteria, F certainly appears to satisfy the third requirement. She has missed half of a year's schooling; as a 17-year-old, she is at an important age for choosing a career; her father has incurred the expense of hiring her a private tutor; and the private tutor has confirmed that she has the ability to study medicine. Thus F may seek compensation for the UK's failure to implement this directive.

Should the UK remain in breach of EC law, the Commission could refer this case to the ECJ (EC Treaty, Art. 169). The UK would be bound to comply with the judgment of the Court, and if it failed to do so a fine would be imposed by the ECJ (EC Treaty, Art. 171, as amended by the Maastricht Treaty on European Union 1992). Since the Commission's enforcement action (Art. 169) cannot be utilised by individuals, F's main remedy is likely to be that the directive is directly effective.

Analysis

(a) This is a long question which raises a number of different points that clearly need to be dealt with in some sort of logical order. In so doing, the material has, again, been structured according to the parties involved, dealing with Ral in part (a) and Fay in part (b). In part (a) there are three main issues:

(i)   whether R can rely on the 1985 Act of Parliament;
(ii)   whether R can challenge the EC Regulation; and
(iii) whether R can avail himself of any remedies under the ECHR.

In Part (b) the issues are easier to spot. They are mainly concerned with the question of whether Fay can invoke the directive in the UK courts to legitimise her wearing of a kap in school. As has been stressed throughout this book, it is imperative that your answer is structured clearly. The strength of this answer is that it separates the issues by using a logical structure and does not get swamped by the sheer volume of available material.

(b) The IRAC method, explained earlier, has also been used in the answer. It can be illustrated if we look at part (a) (i) dealing with whether R can rely on the 1985 Act of Parliament. In the first paragraph, the answer identifies the main issue in part (a). The relevant rules of law are then covered in the next two paragraphs, with paragraph 2 focusing on the position in Europe and paragraph 3 concentrating on that in the UK. Having explained the law in detail, paragraph 4 demonstrates its application to the relevant facts, and the answer analyses R's various legal options. The answer is rounded off with a conclusion: R is unlikely to find the available legal remedies of any use. This same IRAC approach is used in the rest of parts (a) and (b).

(c) As mentioned earlier in this book, resist the temptation to be led by cases (see p. 30). An answer where every sentence starts off with the words, 'In the case of . . .', or in which unnecessary time is devoted to the facts of a case, suggests that you are being controlled by the material rather than vice versa. Note that while a considerable number of cases are cited, it is only the constitutionally significant *R* v *Secretary of State for Transport, ex parte Factortame Ltd* [1990] 2 All ER 85 which warrants detailed analysis.

(d) In many public law courses there are problem questions which take the form of a conflict between an Act of the UK Parliament and a piece of Community legislation. In this question, R is hoping to invoke an Act of Parliament against an EC Regulation, while F is seeking to rely on an EC Directive. In answering such questions, it is important to keep in mind the

differences between regulations and directives. A regulation is 'directly applicable' (Art. 189, EC Treaty), meaning that it is intended to take immediate effect
without the need for further implementation by the state. Thus regulations need
not be re-enacted in national legislation, but must be legally accepted as they
are. By contrast, directives are capable of creating rights which can be enforced
in national courts. In order to determine whether a directive does in fact create
such rights and is what lawyers call 'directly effective', you should ascertain
whether the directive is sufficiently clear, precise and unconditional to be
directly effective (factors of relevance here would be, say, the nature, wording
and background of the directive: *Van Duyn* v *Home Office* [1974] ECR 1337).
Following on from this you should ask yourself three questions:

(i)   Has the time limit of the directive expired? As was pointed out in the
answer, a directive cannot be directly effective until the time limit for
implementation has passed (*Pubblico Ministero* v *Ratti* [1979] ECR 1629).
However, it should be noted that the ECJ has held that a directive may still be
directly effective even when it has been implemented by a state (*Verbond Van
Nederlandse Ondernemigen (VNO)* (Case 51/76) (1977)).

(ii)   Is the direct effect 'vertical' (i.e., does it apply to obligations which
an individual can enforce against a state) or is it 'horizontal' (i.e., are the rights
of a type which individuals can enforce against private bodies or other
individuals)? This distinction is important since it would seem that directives
may have direct effect only against state bodies and not against private bodies
or individuals (*Marshall* v *Southampton and S.W. Hampshire AHA* [1986] QB
401, ECJ). Difficulties arise in questions where it is unclear whether a particular
decision is that of a state body, though in this question the obvious presence of
a public body (the Local Education Authority would satisfy the test for this set
out in *Foster* v *British Gas* [1991] 2 AC 306, HL) indicates that this is a case
of vertical direct effect.

(iii)   Can an individual seek compensation for the state's failure to
implement the directive? This question should be answered using the three-part
Francovich test, outlined in the answer.

If you look carefully at the suggested answer, these questions have been asked.
Of course, this is not the definitive guide to tackling problem questions on
directives. Other questions could be asked, in a different order, but the approach
adopted here will provide your answer with a tight structure and ensure that the
key issues are addressed.

(e)   Following on from what was said in chapter 1 about getting down to the
job at hand as quickly as possible (see pp. 12–14), it is worth pointing out that
the answer does not waste time dwelling on irrelevant issues. For example,
when students answer questions on EC law, some spend a disproportionate
amount of time writing long introductions about the history or institutions of

the Community. In answering the kind of question above, such an introduction is simply unnecessary. Similarly, the answer does not waste words describing the ECHR, instead it immediately focuses on how R may invoke the Treaty to achieve redress.

(f) The question asks the student to advise R and F. You may want to consider not just their legal options, but also any possible political options (since in this area of constitutional law the individual may often have to resort to political remedies). Since R seems unable to avail himself of any effective legal remedy in the UK, the answer includes some political remedies. Note, however, that in these questions you should proceed to discuss political remedies only after having discussed the complainant's legal options.

Note

It is important to realise that not every problem question in the area of constitutional law will take the same form as the question concerning Ral and Fay (i.e., they will not necessarily focus almost exclusively on *legal* issues). Since anyone who has ever studied public law will be aware, there are certain principles which underpin the British constitution (e.g., constitutional conventions, the rule of law, and so on). These principles are essentially *political* rather than legal. Thus, political remedies are often as important for individuals with grievances as those formally provided for by the courts.

As noted earlier, it is possible that a student of public law will be forced to tackle a problem question on these principles of the British constitution. In practice the likelihood of this may depend on the nature of your public law course. Some tutors tend to set only essay questions on this area: others are willing to examine using problem questions (your course co-ordinator will be able to tell you the sorts of questions you can legitimately expect).

When problem questions are set covering constitutional principles, they sometimes cause examinees difficulties. For example, when facing a problem question on devolution, ministerial responsibility or a hung Parliament, the student is forced to consider political rather than legal remedies. Without the reassuringly familiar legal rules to rely on, some students may feel intimidated by such problem questions. Yet in this area the techniques which have been relied upon throughout the book in relation to strictly legal issues can once again be successfully applied to those issues which are essentially political. This is illustrated by the following problem question.

Question

Mandy has been the victim of a serious sexual assault. She was attacked in the street at 2 am after deciding to walk home by herself from a party, following a row with her boyfriend. Mandy was later found dazed and bleeding by a Police Officer. She was immediately rushed to hospital where she was detained for three nights. As a result of the attack she has been receiving specialist counselling for the past six months.

At the trial, in the High Court, of her alleged attacker, the judge, Blythe J, sat with his eyes closed for much of the time. At one point he even appeared to be snoring. In his summing up to the jury, Blythe J addressed the issues and then added: 'Young women should not go out alone late at night. In so doing the victim (who appears not to have suffered any lasting ill effects) was asking for trouble. In this case there has been a great deal of contributory negligence.' Thirty minutes later the defendant was acquitted.

Mandy is particularly incensed by the judge's behaviour and comments. She comes to you for advice.

In answering this question the IRAC technique will again be employed.

Answer

The issue here is one of judicial accountability. Whether a High Court judge may be disciplined, forced to resign or apologise. **[The answer starts off by simply identifying the main issue (the fact that you are to advise Mandy who is 'particularly incensed' by the judge's comments tells us that the answer is about the accountability of judges, as opposed to crimes against women).]** High Court judges are appointed by the Crown on the advice of the Lord Chancellor (Supreme Court Act 1981, s. 10). They hold office during good behaviour and can only be removed by the Queen after a Resolution is passed by both Houses of Parliament (Supreme Court Act 1981, s. 11(3)). Under common law, a judge is protected for anything said in his or her judicial capacity in a court of law (*Scott* v *Stansfield* (1868)), while the Crown is immune from liability for the actions of a judge participating in the judicial process (Crown Proceedings Act 1947, s. 2(5)). **[The relevant constitutional rules have been identified and outlined. Note how the answer refers only to the question of High Court judges – this is all that is required. Thus it does not waste time discussing how inferior judges (e.g., circuit judges) may be removed from office by the Lord Chancellor under the Courts Act 1971, s. 17(4).]**

Mandy (M) appears to have two separate complaints: that the judge failed to pay proper attention to the case; and that he made inappropriate comments about female victims of crime. In the past judges have been criticised for falling asleep and paying inadequate attention to proceedings in court (*R* v *Edworthy* (1961)). Similarly the judge's comments about women 'asking for trouble' are inappropriate and arguably incompatible with his holding office 'during good behaviour'.

In seeking redress, M may wish to draw public attention to the judge's comments about women, while at the same time preserving her anomimity. Thus she might wish to enlist the support of a pressure group (e.g., a women's group). M and her supporters appear to have at least two remedies. They may either petition the Lord Chancellor, or seek to have the judge dismissed by Parliament.

The first option is to petition the Lord Chancellor who could quietly censure the judge. Private pressure might lead Blythe J to apologise or agree that he will no longer hear any more cases involving sex crimes (e.g., in 1993 Judge Prosser agreed not to try any more rape cases after his comment, that the teenage victim of a rape should be given £500 by her attacker for a holiday, caused a public furore). However, if the

Lord Chancellor considers that the judicial misconduct is particularly serious, he could issue a formal public rebuke. The Lord Chancellor issued such a statement in 1982 after a trial judge's comment that a female hitch hiker (who had been raped) was contributorily negligent. It is rare for a Lord Chancellor to censure a judge publicly. However, such a course of action could lead to Blythe J's resignation, or might facilitate his removal from office by Parliament.

The second option is possible in theory but is extremely unlikely in practice. It is almost inconceivable that M could succeed in persuading both Houses of Parliament to dismiss Blythe J for misconduct. There are no published guidelines for what judicial 'good behaviour' means, and a High Court judge was permitted to remain in office in 1975, even though he was found guilty of a drink-driving offence. The last judge to have been removed from office by means of a resolution from both Houses was Jonah Barrington in 1830. In that case Barrington had misappropriated money and at the time of the resolution had effectively retired as a judge. But even if a resolution was proposed in Parliament, precise charges would have to be formulated; and in the absence of any clear precedents these charges might be difficult to draft. In addition, since the issue here is Blythe J's removal from office the judge should be accorded the opportunity of a fair hearing in accordance with the rules of natural justice (*Ridge v Baldwin* (1964)). Thus the whole process is likely to be time-consuming and expensive. [In this part of the answer, the relevant rules have been applied to the facts of the case. It is suggested that M may obtain redress from two possible sources: the Lord Chancellor and Parliament. Although there is very little statutory authority or case law in this area, there are still plenty of authorities to support the answer.]

M's best course of action would appear to be to contact sympathetic MPs (though not Ministers, who by convention are expected to refrain from criticising judges or their decisions). It is a Parliamentary rule that individual backbench MPs may criticise judges only when debating a substantive critical motion. Thus a successful campaign by M's supporters might lead to the introduction of a motion calling for the dismissal of Blythe J. While this would almost certainly fail, it might put sufficient pressure on him to force him to apologise or resign. [This is a simple conclusion: it ties together some of the points which were made earlier. It is also practical in that it notes that M's chances of success ultimately depend on her availing herself of political remedies.]

2. CIVIL LIBERTIES

A typical civil liberties question to be found on public law exam papers will involve the topic of police powers. When considering such questions you might be well advised to keep in mind the following three questions:

(a) Has the police officer a legal power to act in this situation? If so, what does the power consist of (i.e., is it statute based, e.g., Police and Criminal Evidence Act (PACE) 1984, or is it a common law power, e.g., breach of the peace)?

(b) If the police officer has a power to act, is he or she lawfully exercising that power? (Note how often in PACE 1984, a police officer's power is limited by the proviso that it must be exercised reasonably.)

(c)   What safeguards does the individual have? For example, outside the police station, when a stop and search is made, the police officer is under an obligation to convey certain information to the suspect (s. 2(2), (3), PACE 1984). Similarly, inside the police station the individual has the right to consult privately with a lawyer (s. 58, PACE 1984).

Having asked yourself these three questions, as you proceed to write your conclusion, you should ask a final question:

(d)   Has the suspect any remedies (e.g., a later civil action, for assault, false imprisonment etc.)?

We will use this framework and the earlier-mentioned IRAC technique to answer the following question:

Question

PC Dibble and PC Duff are on a foot patrol at 3 am, in a residential area of Grampton. They receive a call to attend a dispute at a nearby house. As they approach the house, they hear a lot of shouting, screaming and the sound of breaking glass. The front door is open, and as they walk up to it they are confronted by Rocky, who is six foot tall and of a muscular build. He is very angry, smells strongly of alcohol, and screams at them that they are not entering his house. Cowering behind him is Walter, who has two black eyes, ripped clothing, a bleeding nose and is in a state of distress. Walter invites the officers into the house, saying that he would like to talk to them. The officers try to push past Rocky. He objects, picks up PC Dibble and throws him into the garden, as a result of which Dibble receives severe bruising. PC Duff summons assistance, and within seconds a van load of officers arrive and drag Rocky into the van, injuring his face in the process. PC Duff tells him that he is taking him to the police station 'to help with enquiries', and he is driven away in the police van.

Suddenly Angie, Rocky's girlfriend, appears from the house. She stands in the road in front of the police van, preventing it from moving and screaming and shouting obscenities at the top of her voice. PC Duff warns her to desist or else she will be arrested. Angie continues to scream. Soon a number of lights come on in nearby houses and it is obvious that she has woken some of her neighbours. Angie is arrested and placed in the police van.

Meanwhile PC Duff returns to the house and searches every room in case 'there is anything that could be evidence'. As a result of the search, he finds a minute quantity of cannabis in Rocky's bedroom.

Discuss.

Answer

The entry of the Police officers and Rocky's response
The first issue is whether the police may lawfully enter the house. One factor to consider is whether Walter has the authority to invite the officers inside. **[Using the**

IRAC method, the first issue is addressed.] At common law a police officer may enter premises with the express or implied permission of the owner (*Davis v Lisle* (1936)). If Walter is the owner/occupier, the entry is lawful; similarly, entry is permissible if Walter and Rocky are joint owners/occupiers (*R v Thornley* (1981, CA)), and even if Walter is a co-occupier he may be able to grant entry (*R v Lamb* (1990)).

Irrespective of the above, the police have a common law power to enter public or private premises to prevent or deal with a breach of the peace: the rule in *Thomas v Sawkins* (1935), retained in s. 17(6), Police and Criminal Evidence Act (PACE) 1984. Mere rowdiness of itself will not constitute a breach of the peace – instead breach of the peace is limited to situations where violence has occurred or the likelihood of it occurring is imminent (*R v Howell* (1981, CA)). **[The relevant *rules* of law relating to common law powers of entry are explained.]** Thus, Walter's black eyes, torn clothes and bleeding nose demonstrate that violence (an essential prerequisite of breach of the peace) has occurred. The fact that this violence took place in a private home is no defence, since a breach of the peace can take place on private premises for the purpose of entitling a constable on reasonable grounds to make an arrest (*McConnell v CC Greater Manchester* (1990, CA)). And a police officer has an independent right under common law to remain on premises if he or she reasonably anticipates a breach of the peace on those premises (*Lamb v DPP* (1989)). Walter's condition, plus the sounds of shouting, screaming and breaking glass, appear to provide the police officers with reasonable grounds to so act. **[Application of the law to the facts, and conclusion.]**

In addition to their common law powers, the police officers may rely on s. 17, PACE 1984. **[Issue]** They seem to have a number of options. First, as mentioned earlier, the police retain their power of entry to prevent a breach of the peace (s. 17(6)). Secondly, relying on s. 17(1)(e), the police officers might argue that they wish to enter the premises to save life or limb (e.g., Walter's), or to prevent serious damage to property due to Rocky's enraged state (e.g., breaking glass). Thirdly, it is possible that the police have a power of entry under s. 17(1)(b) to arrest for an arrestable offence, as defined in s. 24, PACE 1984. This would be exercisable (s. 17(2)(a)) only if the police had reasonable grounds for believing that the person they were seeking (here Rocky) was on the premises (he was). **[Relevant rules of law relating to PACE, s. 17.]** In view of Walter's black eyes, bleeding nose, ripped clothing and distressed state, it appears that there may have been an assault, occasioning actual bodily harm (s. 47, Offences Against the Persons Act (OAPA) 1861) or grievous bodily harm (s. 20, OAPA 1861). Both of these are arrestable offences (s. 24(1)(b)). The police might also seek to invoke the wide powers of arrest under s. 24(6), which stipulates that where there are reasonable grounds for suspecting that an arrestable offence has been committed, an arrest can be made without warrant of anyone whom there are reasonable grounds for suspecting is guilty of that offence. Blood on Rocky's hands would indicate this and the test for reasonable grounds is objective (*Castorina v CC of Surrey* (1988, CA)). **[Application of the law to the facts.]**

These powers, read with the facts, tend to suggest that the entry of the police officers is lawful. Thus, assuming that the officers are acting lawfully, Rocky's actions may mean that he has assaulted a constable in the execution of his duty, contrary to s. 51(1), Police Act 1964. However, on being arrested Rocky must be informed of the fact and the grounds for the arrest, either at the time or as soon as possible thereafter

(s. 28). It should have been made clear to Rocky that he was being arrested (*R* v *Brosch* (1988, CA)), so that merely being told that he is 'helping with enquiries' is too vague.

Since he has been unlawfully detained, Rocky may be entitled to use reasonable force to escape (*Kenlin* v *Gardiner* (1967)). Picking up PC Dibble and throwing him into the garden certainly does not seem to be reasonable. What is less clear is whether the officers used reasonable force in restraining Rocky, who is tall and well built. The 'dragging' of Rocky and the injury to his face suggests that unreasonable force was used and certainly excludes his voluntary attendance at the police station (s. 29, PACE 1984). [**Conclusion.**]

The arrest of Angie

The next issue is whether Angie can be lawfully arrested. [**A new issue.**] Angie has been arrested for shouting in a residential area in the middle of the night. The grounds for arrest could be behaviour 'within the hearing or sight' of people 'likely to be caused harassment, alarm or distress' (Public Order Act (POA) 1986, s. 5(1). The fact that lights come on in nearby houses might indicate that this is established. And even if only the police officers witnessed Angie screaming then, according to *DPP* v *Orum* (1988), they too are capable of being caused harassment, alarm or distress for the purposes of s. 5. [**Rule.**] Thus, Angie may be arrested under POA 1986, s. 5(4). She is unlikely to be able to rely on the two available defences to this offence: (i) that she lacks *mens rea* (s. 6(4)) (there is no indication that she does); and (ii) that her behaviour is reasonable (s. 5(3)(c)) (screaming obscenities at 3 am in a residential district seems unreasonable). By standing in front of the police van in the road, Angie may also be wilfully obstructing the highway (Highways Act 1980, s. 137). However, it is more likely that Angie is committing the offence of obstructing the police in the execution of their duty (Police Act 1964, s. 51(3)), for which the officers have the power to arrest for obstruction (*Wershoff* v *MPC* (1978)). [**Application and Conclusion.**]

The search of the house

Another issue to be discussed is whether by returning to the house and searching it, PC Duff is acting illegally. [**Issue.**] A police officer may enter a house by warrant, statute, or consent. [**Rule.**] There is no evidence that it has been authorised by a warrant (s. 8, PACE 1984), or by Walter. And even presupposing that Walter has sufficient authority, his consent must be given in writing before the search takes place, with the police officer satisfied that Walter is in a position to give consent (Code B, 4.1). Since this has not happened, the entry would appear to be prima facie unlawful. In addition, the breach of the Code may affect the admissibility of the cannabis seized in later court proceedings (s. 67(10), PACE 1984) and the court may choose to exclude it (s. 78, PACE 1984). [**Application and Conclusion.**]

Neither can PC Duff's entry be justified under s. 18, PACE 1984. [**Issue.**] This section provides that an officer can enter premises only if there are reasonable grounds for suspecting that there is present evidence in relation to an arrestable offence he or she is investigating. [**Rule.**] It is difficult to see how this might be the case in the problem; and even if such a search were permitted, it has not been authorised in writing by an officer of at least the rank of inspector (s. 18(4), PACE 1984). [**Application.**]

Presumably PC Duff seizes the cannabis under s. 19(3), PACE 1984 to prevent it from being concealed or destroyed. However, he must have been lawfully in the house to seize any items (s. 19(1), PACE 1984). Since this is in doubt, Rocky will hope that the court will exercise its discretion under s. 78, PACE 1984, to exclude the evidence of the minute quantity of cannabis, on the ground that it was unfairly obtained (*R* v *Khan* (1994, CA)).

Irrespective of the success of this argument, Rocky may consider bringing a civil action against the police. The failure lawfully to arrest Rocky could lead to a civil actions for false imprisonment while unreasonable force in his detention could provide the basis for an action for assault. Finally, an action may lie for trespass to property (in relation to the later, unlawful search). Rocky would sue the Chief Constable of the force, but any damages would be paid by his Police Authority (s. 48, Police Act 1964).

Lastly, even if these actions are not successful, Rocky and Angie could complain to the Police Complaints Authority (s. 83, PACE 1984) about the actions of the officers in this scenario. While statistically their chances of success are low, it is possible that disciplinary charges would be brought against those officers who flouted the rules in PACE 1984 and the Code of Practice. [**Conclusion.**]

Analysis

(a)   In order to answer this question, a student must first decide whether the police officers have the power to enter the house. The answer highlights three possibilities:

(i)   the right of a co-occupier or joint owner to grant permission;
(ii)   common law police powers to enter to deal with a breach of the peace;
(iii) section 17 of PACE 1984.

The first possibility, (i), is the most obvious. The fact that Walter is in the house at 3 am would imply that he resides there (it may also be significant that the door is open and were this not his house Walter might have 'escaped'). On the other hand, Rocky refers to it as 'his house' and the drugs are found in 'Rocky's' bedroom. Further speculation is unnecessary. Instead, cite the relevant case law, pulling out these the noteworthy facts (which, by the way, should have been brought out in the answer). The details here are left deliberately vague. This is for the student to proceed to discuss the other options available to the police officers in deciding whether they can lawfully enter the house.

The second possibility, (ii), is the power of the police to prevent or to deal with a breach of the peace. The fact that most public law textbooks deal with the breach of the peace in their chapters on public order (and not in the police powers section) occasionally deceives a few students into thinking that breach of the peace could not possibly be relevant in a question which is ostensibly on police powers. Such an idea is fallacious and shows the danger of ignoring 'the big picture'. As you will have observed, significant public order issues arise later in the question. This should serve as a warning to 'question spotters'. If you gamble on leaving out an area of your course – always a dangerous option – try to ensure that it is unrelated to those areas on which you are hoping to rely.

The third possibility, (iii), is that the police officers may invoke other provisions in s. 17, PACE 1984 to enter the house. The sheer length of s. 17 can intimidate some students and it is not unknown for the weaker ones (who, while in the exam hall, have the benefit of a statute book containing PACE 1984) to copy out as part of their answer large parts of s. 17 without detailed explanation. Such a course of action is, not surprisingly, unproductive. As noted earlier, where a statute book is provided, you will not receive credit for repeating the relevant statutory section – in fact all that you are doing is drawing your lack of knowledge to the examiner's attention. Instead, relate the appropriate statutory provisions to the facts of the question.

(b)   The main advantage of a method such as the IRAC or the four-step formula is that it will ensure that your answer has a good, clear structure. Students are often tempted to abandon such an approach in the rush to put pen to paper. From the above answer, you will have noticed that the first two parts of the suggested four-part formula – the existence of a power and the use of that power – overlap. In the same way, parts (c) and (d) (the individual's safeguards and remedies) tend to cross over. For example, in this scenario, s. 28, PACE 1984 (information to be conveyed on arrest) appears not to have been complied with. Because Rocky has not been given the grounds and reason for his arrest, the police officers lose the shield of the law. Thus Rocky can bring a civil action for false imprisonment, seeking damages from the period when first detained to the time he was notified of his arrest. Similarly, the fact that the police officers 'drag Rocky into the van, injuring his face in the process', suggests the use of unreasonable force and an action for assault. The principle of vicarious liability means that the Chief Constable of the relevant force will be the defendant. These are rather obvious points, but it is surprising how many students fail to raise them. One possible explanation is that many examinees assume that since such civil actions come within the framework of the law of tort, they could not possibly be relevant in a public law exam. Of course, a detailed analysis of the possible tortious issues is not necessary, yet civil actions have increasingly been seen as effective remedies to which individuals aggrieved by police misconduct may resort. Your inclusion of this issue will suggest that you have a good overall understanding of public law.

(c)   The introduction of Angie into the problem question raises issues of public order law. Note how the answer did not limit itself solely to the Public Order Act 1986. Instead it draws upon the two other sources of law relevant to this area: common law powers (e.g., breach of the peace), and other statutory powers (e.g., Highways Act 1980). Nevertheless, the Public Order Act 1986 is an important piece of legislation and if you answer a question on this area you must have a good working knowledge of it (as well as the more recent Criminal

Justice and Public Order Act 1994 – which was not relevant for the purposes of the present question). Here a competent student will identify the power of arrest – it is significant that Angie was arrested only after the police officer told her to stop screaming and swearing, and warned her that she could be arrested. This satisfies s. 5(4), Public Order Act 1986, which provides that where a police officer warns a person to cease engaging in 'offensive conduct' and that person fails to stop, the police officer then has the power to make an arrest.

(d) Lastly, since some of the facts in this question are quite unclear, the suggested answer raises a number of different possibilities. It can reasonably be assumed that the examiner deliberately left parts of the question vague, so that the student is free to explore a range of different options. The fact that the question asks you to 'discuss', rather than a more specific instruction, (e.g., advise Rocky), would tend to confirm this.

3. JUDICIAL REVIEW

One possible strategy in approaching judicial review problem questions is to start by asking yourself four questions:

(a) Is this the decision of a body which is, in principle, subject to judicial review (i.e., is it a public law matter)?

(b) If so, has the applicant complied with the procedural requirements for judicial review (e.g., *locus standi*, time limits etc.)?

(c) Are there grounds for seeking judicial review (e.g., illegality, irrationality and procedural impropriety)?

(d) What legal remedies may the applicant invoke?

This technique can be illustrated by looking at the following question:

Question

An Act of Parliament has granted local authorities the power to acquire land compulsorily to build sports facilities in areas where there is a 'definite need' for these facilities. Any such action can only be taken under this Act after a period of public consultation following a majority vote of councillors in a full Council meeting. It must also be subject to the approval of the Minister for Sport.

In February 1996, Frank received notice that Greytown District Council Planning Committee had decided that his house was to be compulsorily purchased and demolished to facilitate the building of a large leisure complex, which was to include an Olympic size swimming pool. The Minister for Sport approved the proposed development.

Frank complains that there is already an indoor swimming pool three miles from his house. While this pool is not of Olympic size, it is busy only at weekends. Frank also wonders if it is relevant that the son of the Chairman of the Council, who is a well-known swimmer, published a letter in a local paper a year earlier, in which he complained that he had difficulty training as there were no Olympic size swimming pools in that area.

Advise Frank.

Answer

Procedural requirements
Frank's application must be brought within three months from the date on which the decision he is seeking to challenge was taken (RSC, Order 53, rule 4; *R v Stratford-on-Avon DC, ex parte Jackson* (1985, CA)). Since judicial review is available only where public law issues are concerned, Frank is fortunate that in this scenario the administrative authorities (the Council and the Minister) are clearly public law bodies. To seek leave for judicial review, the applicant must have a sufficient interest in the matter to which the application relates (Supreme Court Act, s. 31(3)). Since it is Frank's house which is to be compulsorily purchased, he certainly appears to have standing or *locus standi*. Assuming that leave for judicial review is granted, the court will turn to examine the substantive basis of Frank's challenge. In the *GCHQ* case (1984, HL), Lord Diplock defined the grounds for judicial review using a threefold classification of illegality, procedural impropriety, and irrationality.

Illegality
Illegality covers situations where administrative authorities have made jurisdictional errors or have acted *ultra vires*. Here Frank will claim that the local authority (LA) appears to have exceeded its powers and has acted *ultra vires* (illegally) in two respects. First, substantive *ultra vires*. The Act enables the LA compulsorily to acquire land to build sports facilities only. However, the LA proposes to construct a leisure complex. Frank will argue that this is a different enterprise from that provided in the Act. Since 'leisure' implies the construction of shops, cinemas and restaurants, this may mean that the LA is exceeding the power delegated to it by the statute (*A-G v Fulham Corp* (1921)). The LA, on the other hand, might contend that a leisure complex is reasonably incidental to the legislation (*A-G v Great Eastern Railway* (1880, CA)). However, Frank could respond that the 'reasonably incidental' principle tends to be narrowly construed (*McCarthy and Stone v Richmond* (1992, HL)).

Secondly, Frank may claim that there has been an unauthorised delegation of power. This is the principle that where a statute grants a power to a particular administrative body, that authority may not be delegated to another, unless provided for or authorised by the Act of Parliament (*Barnard v National Dock Labour Board* (1953, CA)). Therefore Frank could argue that the LA has improperly delegated its power to its planning committee. On the other hand, the LA may respond by pointing out that in local government, councils have wide powers to delegate their functions to committees and sub-committees (Local Government Act 1972, s. 101). The legitimacy of this delegation will ultimately turn on the actual wording of the Act. Whatever the outcome on this issue, there would in any case appear to exist procedural impropriety.

Procedural impropriety
Since there is no indication that the LA has complied with the specific procedure in the Act of ensuring public consultation, or that the compulsory purchase has been authorised by a majority vote of councillors in a full council meeting, there seems to

have been a procedural irregularity. The courts have moved from only distinguishing between mandatory and directory requirements (*Howard* v *Bodington* (1877)), so that where there is non-compliance with a procedural requirement they take into account all of the circumstances in determining whether it would be fair to set aside the decision (*R* v *Secretary of State for Social Services, ex parte A.M.A.* (1986)). Thus Frank will argue that since there is a lot at stake for him and third parties such as his neighbours (e.g., losing their homes), the failure to consult and comply with the statutory procedure means that the LA's decision should be set aside (*Lee* v *D.E.S.* (1967)). This is a strong argument, and it is difficult to see how the LA could convincingly raise a defence that Frank is not prejudiced by the LA's non-compliance with the procedural requirements (*Main* v *Swansea CC* (1985, CA)).

Procedural impropriety also includes judge-made rules of procedural fairness and natural justice. Thus even if Frank is unsuccessful in making this submission, he has another argument: natural justice. Traditionally the courts divided the rules of natural justice into two categories: (i) the rule against bias; and (ii) the right to a fair hearing. Notwithstanding the fact that the courts tend now to emphasise a duty to act fairly (*Ridge* v *Baldwin* (1964, HL)), Frank may seek to rely on the traditional two principles of natural justice.

The fact that the son of the Council Chairman is a keen swimmer who has publicly called for the construction of an Olympic size swimming pool, obviously creates the impression of bias. Frank will rely on the principle that 'justice may not only be done but should . . . be seen to be done' (Lord Hewart in *R* v *Sussex Justices, ex parte McCarthy* (1924)). He will argue that the Council Chairman as a man of rank could unfairly influence Council policy (*Metropolitan Properties Ltd* v *Lannon* (1969, CA)) – even if he took no part in the Council's decision (*R* v *Hendon RDC* (1933)) – so there is a 'real danger' of bias (*R* v *Gough* (1993, HL)). Thus unless the Council can make a strong case otherwise (e.g., that it was Council policy to build the complex long before the Chairman took his position and his son wrote the letter, or that the Council was elected on a pledge to build an Olympic swimming pool or that the Chairman had no real influence over Council policy), there would appear to be bias.

Since Frank's house is to be demolished for the construction of the new complex, he can also argue that he should be accorded a fair hearing (*Cooper* v *Wandsworth Board of Works* (1863)). On the facts, there is no indication that Frank has been given this opportunity. The right to a fair hearing should depend on the consequences of the decision to the individual (*Ridge* v *Baldwin* (1964)). Normally neither an oral hearing nor legal representation are automatic ingredients of a fair hearing (*R* v *Board of Visitors, Maze Prison, ex parte Hone* (1988, HL)). However, Frank could argue that since he has a lot to lose, he should be accorded additional rights, because the test for fairness depends on the circumstances of every case (*Lloyd* v *McMahon* (1987, HL)).

Irrationality
As well as illegality and procedural impropriety, Frank can challenge the decision to demolish his house on the remaining ground of irrationality. Frank can argue that there is no 'definite need' for either an Olympic pool or such a complex; that no reasonable council would embark on such an enterprise when there is already a pool in the locality (*Wednesbury* (1948, HL)); and that such a decision is perverse and lacks logic (*GCHQ* case (1984)).

The Council might try to justify its decision on the ground that the existing pool is unsafe or too small to cater for local needs. Yet Frank could respond that rather than demolishing his house to build a new pool, it would seem logical to refurbish and expand the existing pool. Ultimately the legitimacy of this decision will turn on the facts. Thus if the LA can show that its new complex is being designed to respond to a population increase (e.g., new housing estates are being built or new businesses are coming to the area) then that may well be enough to rebut the presumption that the decision is unreasonable. Certainly Frank should be mindful of the fact that the courts are usually slow to strike down administrative decisions as irrational (*R* v *Secretary of State for Defence, ex parte Sancto* (1992)). After all, Lord Diplock (in the *GCHQ* case 1984) defined irrationality narrowly to cover a decision so outrageous 'that no sensible person' could have reached it.

Remedies

Having invoked these grounds for review, it seems very likely that Frank's legal challenge will be successful. While remembering that all public law remedies are discretionary, Frank would be well advised to seek a prohibitory injunction (preventing the LA from compulsorily purchasing his house). This would ensure that in the meantime his house is not demolished (*AG* v *Fulham Corp* (1921)). Since the Planning Committee has already taken the decision to purchase and demolish his house, Frank should also seek an order of certiorari to quash the decision (as opposed to prohibition which is sought to prevent such actions). Frank may also seek a declaration that the Committee's decision to make the order is null and void. While not legally enforceable, such declarations are usually obeyed and have been issued in response to unreasonable planning conditions (*Hall* v *Shoreham UDC* (1964, CA)).

Lastly it should be observed that if Frank was unsuccessful in seeking leave to apply for judicial review, he has two further remedies: he could invoke the Parliamentary Commissioner for Administration concerning the Minister's approval of the proposed development (Parliamentary Commissioner for Administration Act 1967, s. 5), or the Commissioners for Local Administration (Local Government Act 1974, s. 26) who investigate complaints of local authority maladministration.

Analysis

You should consider the following points in planning how to answer a judicial review problem question:

(a)   The suggested four part micro structure to be applied in these questions, will provide a useful model for marshalling your arguments. You may, however, be wondering about the order of the questions. It is important to note that this order is not accidental. The reason why it might be wise to discuss the issue of the availability of judicial review before looking at the grounds on which the relevant decision can be reviewed, may be explained by comparing the importance of remedies in this area to that of private law. For example, in subjects such as contract or tort, it must first be established whether the plaintiff has been legally wronged by the defendant; only then is it worth considering the availability of any remedies. However, an applicant for judicial review should consider the question of whether judicial review offers legal remedies at the earliest opportunity. The reason for this is simple – no matter how strong the substantive case for judicial review may be (e.g., Lord Diplock's so-called three 'i's – illegality, impropriety, and irrationality), a successful application for judicial review must comply with the correct procedure. In other words, even if the applicant has been adversely affected by a decision which is obviously illegal or irrational, he or she may lose if he or she has failed to satisfy the *locus standi* or time limit requirements. Thus, the suggested answer commences with a brief outline of the procedural hurdles Frank must overcome.

(b)   So what overall proportion of your answer should each part of the four question model cover? Ultimately the weight which you attach to each of the elements of the proposed model will depend on both the wording of the problem question you are tackling and its instructions. Here guidance is provided by the facts of the question, because the decision has been taken by a Minister and a local authority. Since there is no uncertainty about whether the relevant administrative authority is a public law body or whether it is exercising a public function (see *R* v *Panel on Take-Overs and Mergers, ex parte Datafin plc* [1987] 1 All ER 564, where the Court of Appeal, in offering guidelines as to what is a public law body, held that the classification of a body as public has to do with the source of its power and also its functions), you should avoid a detailed analysis of what exactly is a public law issue. It is simply not necessary. Similarly, the close connection between Frank and the compulsory purchase and demolition of his house, suggests that satisfying the *locus standi* requirement is not a problem. Again, anything other than a brief reference to this would be unnecessary. Lastly, since the question does not ask for a description or an analysis of the procedure to be employed when applying for judicial review, its inclusion is superfluous. Avoid unnecessary background information. Students who start their answers with a disproportionately long introduction, charting, for example, the history of the Supreme Court Act 1981, or merely describing the Order 53 procedure, can expect little credit. They are more likely to irritate than to impress the examiner, who just wants to see each student answer the question and tackle the relevant legal issues.

(c)   In answering this question, we have used Lord Diplock's 3'i's test (introduced in *CCSU* v *Minister for the Civil Service* [1985] AC 374, referred to in the answer as the *GCHQ* case). It is a useful tool, a sort of 'legal umbrella', which categorises the different grounds for review. As you may have observed when studying judicial review, the classification may be tidy, but it is not perfect. Cases frequently arise which fall into more than one of Lord Diplock's categories and some academics dislike the test as it may erroneously imply that there are only three ways of challenging administrative action. Common sense dictates that if the lecturer on your course has an aversion to the Diplock classification you may be advised to embrace their ideas. However, whatever approach you adopt (and the suggested answer adopts the first one), make sure that you identify and analyse the different grounds for review. Certainly, the alliteration of Lord Diplock's test (the three 'i's), makes it easy to remember;

and the fact that the House of Lords has subsequently endorsed it (*R* v *Secretary of State for the Environment, ex parte Hammersmith and Fulham LBC* [1991] 1 AC 521), makes it not merely a useful, but also an authoritative method for handling the grounds of judicial review.

Lastly, having identified the grounds for review, you should identify Frank's remedies. It is important to match your remedies to the facts and legal issues generated in the question. Sometimes weak students will just list the remedies (mandamus, certiorari, prohibition, injunction, declaration and damages) in note form, without any detailed explanation of which are relevant and why. This 'hit and hope' approach is not likely to fool the examiner. Having identified the appropriate remedies, you should point out that all public law remedies (with the exception of damages) are discretionary – for example, the motives of the applicant may be relevant (*R* v *Commissioners of Customs and Excise, ex parte Cook* [1970] 1 WLR 450) – so that there is no right to a remedy, irrespective of the strength of the merits of his or her case.

(d)   In answering these questions, always bear in mind the nature of judicial review. Judicial review is the power of the High Court to supervise the actions of government bodies applying public law principles. Thus it is important not to confuse or misuse the terms 'appeal' and 'review'. There are significant differences. Appeal proceedings enable the court to change the decision of the body appealed from in a particular case (e.g., in tort, an appeal court can increase the sum of damages to be awarded to the victim of an accident caused by the defendant's negligence). However, review means that the court has only a supervisory jurisdiction (e.g., the supervising court cannot take decisions, it can only quash illegal decisions). Unlike an appeal, which give the court the power to decide whether a decision on appeal was 'right or wrong', judicial review empowers a court only to review whether the decision was 'legal'. Thus judicial review cannot take the place of administrative or political controls on official decisions. It cannot be used to challenge the *merits* of governmental or administrative policy. Only if a decision is unlawful can it be quashed. Therefore the student who writes 'Frank should appeal for judicial review,' is revealing his or her lack of knowledge and understanding of this area.

(e)   Remember that there are some factors, not so far covered, which may restrict the Court's powers of review. Obvious examples of things to look out for are public interest immunity certificates and ouster clauses. Similarly, the reports of the Parliamentary Commissioner for Administration have been held by judges to be immune from review (*R* v *PCA ex parte Dyer* [1994] 1 All ER 375). The fact that none of these areas is relevant to the problem at hand should not detract from their potential importance to any judicial review question you might later have to answer.

(f)   It is axiomatic that a number of judicial review cases are politically controversial. The courts have been asked to answer politically sensitive questions such as: Could the elected Greater London Council lawfully cut the price of travelling on the London Underground (*Bromley* v *GLC* [1983] 1 AC

768)? Could Spanish owners of fishing vessels force the UK Government to allow their ships to fish in British waters pending a ruling from the European Court of Justice (*R* v *Secretary of State for Transport, ex parte Factortame Ltd* [1990] 2 AC 85)? Could the Home Secretary lawfully ban the transmission of words spoken by members of Sinn Fein and other proscribed organisations (*R* v *Secretary of State for the Home Department, ex parte Brind* [1991] 1 AC 696)? Could a ten-year-old girl with cancer require a Health Authority to continue to fund her treatment (*R* v *Cambridge HA, ex parte B* [1995] 2 All ER 129)? Students invariably have their own political views on such decisions, but even though judges may indirectly evaluate the legitimacy of social and political policies, a judicial review problem question is not the appropriate forum for the expression of political sentiment. Avoid partisan political comment in your answers – it is not that your examiner may disagree with you, it is just that he or she will probably find it irrelevant. Of course, essay questions on topics such as proportional representation, or the reform of the Monarchy or the House of Lords are essentially political. Yet although it is inevitable that you will be making explicit political judgments in these answers, you must not become unnecessarily side-tracked by party politics. Avoid soapbox rhetoric at all costs. Remember that you are in a law exam, and whatever leeway you have in answering the question, you will be expected to apply the tools of legal reasoning.

PART B
ESSAY QUESTIONS

Chapter 5

Essay Questions

Unlike legal problem-solving, all law students will have had the opportunity to practise essay writing at some stage of their academic career. Despite this background, many students fail to do justice to themselves simply because of the approach they adopt. Without denying that good essay writing is difficult, it is our view that it can be made easier if you have: (1) the appropriate material upon which to draw; (2) thought about the issues and formulated your ideas *before* the exam, rather than during it; (3) carefully dissected the question; and (4) structured your answer.

1. GATHERING THE APPROPRIATE MATERIAL

In gathering together the appropriate materials you may first want to turn to your lecture notes and the notes you have taken from textbooks. However, these will almost certainly not be enough for most essay answers. Contrary to what you might think (or have been told by students who are more 'advanced' in their studies), the law journal articles that you are asked to read are not the 'icing on the cake'; they are the 'fodder' for your essay answers – they will provide you with arguments for and against various propositions, offer views on how legal disputes should be resolved, present rationales for different legal rules, and so on. Of course, you may not feel able to read *all* the articles set for every tutorial. However, you should read some and, more importantly, you should make sure that you have covered all the most significant ones by the time examinations come round. If you have failed to read the relevant articles you will struggle to write a good essay, simply because your knowledge is limited.

Another good source of material for essay writing is minority judgments. Indeed, if you are pressed for time in preparing for a tutorial and find that you will not be able to read as widely as you would like, you should read the minority judgments. There you should find the arguments of the majority subjected to criticism. That way, you will find out what the law is, as well as any criticisms of the view(s) held by the majority.

2.   FORMULATING YOUR IDEAS

Many students are surprisingly naive when it comes to writing essays. Often they assume that quick thinking in the heat of the exam will be sufficient to score high marks. Although this may be true on certain occasions, as a rule a good essay answer will require considered reflection of the issues involved – something which it is extremely difficult to do in the context of an exam where you are under severe time constraints. Consequently, it is particularly important that you formulate your ideas and views *before* you enter the exam room rather than while you are in it. This approach requires you to put some time aside to *think* about the 'big picture' – how different parts of your course fit together – as well as time to work out your own 'position' on specific issues. If you have done so you will be in a better position to handle the issues raised by the question.

Of course, there will be many issues in law school about which you will care little, if at all. It is the rare law student who spends sleepless nights worrying about whether recklessness in the criminal law should be objective or subjective, or where the boundaries should be set for recovery of damages in negligence. Although it almost goes without saying that if you do not care about *any* of the issues which you encounter in law school you might want to reconsider your reasons for being there, the real point to note is that the examiner is not at all interested in the extent to which you do care about these matters. Rather, the examiner is interested in your powers of analysis, reasoning, and expression as reflected in your willingness and ability to *engage with* a question on a (typically difficult) legal issue.

It is also a good discipline to experiment with writing answers or outlining arguments which support views that you do not necessarily hold. This will help you to see that there is always at least one other point of view.

3.   DISSECTING THE QUESTION

Dissecting the question is a two-stage process. First, you must work out what the question is asking you to do. Then secondly, you need to determine what issues must be addressed in order to do that.

In relation to the first part of this process, questions fall into three basic categories – though there may be some overlaps between and variations on them.

A. *Explain*

This is the simplest type of question which asks you merely to describe or explain something or the relationship between phenomena. For example:

What do you understand by the Rule of Law? What is its constitutional significance?

Is it possible to distinguish between situations where (i) a constitutional convention has been broken and (ii) a constitutional convention has been altered to accommodate changed circumstances?

In what circumstances is there criminal liability for omissions in English law?

A slightly more complex example of this form of question is:

In the light of your understanding of the relationship (or otherwise) between law and morality, explain how you would have decided the appeal to the House of Lords in *Brown* (the sado-masochism case).

B. *Discuss*

More common is the type of question which contains a quotation that expresses a particular point of view about something and then asks you to discuss it. In such questions you are expected both to explain the statement made and to assess whether or not you think it is correct, giving reasons for your answer. For example:

'The electoral system in Britain is, and should be, designed to produce popular government rather than a legislature strictly representative of popular opinion.'

Discuss.

'Until problems in the relationship between the increasingly politicised civil service and Parliament are resolved, Select Committees will be in a weak position to investigate the activities of central government departments.'

Discuss.

Variations on this type of question are: Discuss with reference to . . .; or, Do you agree? For example:

The concept of just deserts defines the boundaries of the extent of permissible punishment in any individual case. Deviation from this norm should not be permitted on utilitarian grounds.

Do you agree?

Another variation on this theme is where you are given two contrasting quotations in response to which you are asked to decide which is the more accurate and why.

C. Critically Evaluate

Such questions usually ask you to assess the success or appropriateness of a particular institution or area of law, as well as to explain what it is. They divide into two sub-categories:

(i)   Evaluation in a vacuum
In this case you must decide for yourself what criteria of assessment should be used. You should ask yourself what is the institution or law? What can or should it be expected to achieve? And, finally, which standards are you using to justify your choice? Remember that there may be multiple or even competing objectives. If this is the case this should be acknowledged and incorporated into your answer – this may be a reason why an institution or the law is not successful. For example:

> Critically evaluate the constitutional position of political parties in the United Kingdom.

> Is the current status of the European Convention on Human Rights in English Law acceptable?

(ii)   Evaluation against standards supplied in the question
Here the bulk of the discussion must take place in the light of the particular criteria identified in the question, but the good student may wish to point out that these are not the only, or most important standards against which the law or institution should be measured. The question itself may ask you, implicitly or explicitly, to assess the importance of the given criteria, through the use of words such as 'sufficient' or 'adequate'. For example:

> To what extent are the rules and principles of judicial review capable of providing clear guidance to public officials as to the boundaries of lawful administrative action?

> Does English law give sufficient protection to people's right to protest?

A variation on these two categories of question might be to ask you to suggest appropriate reforms.

Having worked out what it is you are being asked to do, your answer must also determine what issues you should cover. In order to demonstrate this stage, some of the above questions are used:

The concept of just deserts defines the boundaries of the extent of permissible punishment in any individual case. Deviation from this norm should not be permitted on utilitarian grounds.

Do you agree?

Whatever way you decide to answer this question (agreeing with the quotation or disagreeing with it), the following issues would have to be addressed:

(i)   What is the 'just deserts' theory?
(ii)   What problems exist with the just deserts theory?
(iii)   What do utilitarian grounds mean?
(iv)   Can one justify deviation from the just deserts theory on utilitarian grounds?

Or, if the question is:

In the light of your understanding of the relationship (or otherwise) between law and morality, explain how you would have decided the appeal to the House of Lords in *Brown* (the sado-masochism case).

Then, whatever way you decide to answer this question (pro-*Brown* or anti-*Brown*), the following issues would have to be addressed:

(i)   What were the issues raised by the *Brown* decision?
(ii)   What is the link between law and morality? (Hart/Devlin debate)
(iii)   In what way would that debate influence your decision in *Brown*?

By the same token, if the question is:

'Until problems in the relationship between the increasingly politicised civil service and Parliament are resolved, Select Committees will be in a weak position to investigate the activities of central government departments.'

Discuss

Then, somewhere in your answer, the following issues must be addressed:

(i)   What is the relationship between the civil service and Parliament supposed to be?
(ii)   Why might it be said to be increasingly politicised (and what relevance does this have)?
(iii)   What powers do Select Committees have to investigate the affairs of central government departments?

(iv)   Insofar as they are in a weak position, is that weakness attributable to the problems in the relationship between the civil service and Parliament?
(v)   How might these weaknesses be resolved?

Although points (i)–(v) represent the issues which must be addressed, they should be covered in such a way as to give proper emphasis to the gist of the question – here the focus is on Select Committees (you are being asked about the Civil Service and Parliament as an explanation for the weak position of Select Committees, and this should be reflected in your answer).

Admittedly not all essay questions lend themselves to this sort of dissection, but many do; and it is a useful way of making sure that you answer the question fully.

4.   STRUCTURING AND PRESENTING YOUR MATERIAL EFFECTIVELY

Assuming you have access to the appropriate material, have thought about it, and dissected the question in the appropriate manner suggested above, you must then begin to order your thoughts. As we have just seen, how you should answer an essay question depends very much on the question asked; but whatever form the question takes, the key – as with answering problem questions – is structure. Notwithstanding the different types of essay questions outlined earlier, see pp. 108-110, for the sake of simplicity we divide them into two groups for the purpose of demonstrating the sorts of structural techniques that are available to produce a good answer.

A.   Answers which need only be descriptive

This is the 'Explain' type question, as described above. Here, all you need to do is present your material within a good, clear, tight framework, supported by relevant authority i.e., there is no need to advance an argument. Some of the ways in which material can be marshalled for these purposes have already been touched on. As was mentioned earlier, the most popular method is to outline the general rule and then to list the different exceptions, or some variation on this theme. For example:

Question

In what circumstances is there criminal liability for omissions in English law?

Answer

There is no general principle of liability in English criminal law for failing to act. So, for example, as a general rule no liability will attach to A if she watches B drown in a shallow pond, where rescue would have been easy. However, in a number of instances a failure to act can constitute the *actus reus* of an offence:

(a)   where the definition of the offence actually specifies an omission to act (e.g., failing to file an income tax form when required to do so);
(b)   where a special relationship exists between the parties (e.g., parent/child relationship);
(c)   where a duty has been voluntarily assumed (e.g., *Stone* v *Dobinson* (1977); *Instan* (1893));
(d)   where a duty arises by way of a contract (e.g., *Pitwood* (1902));
(e)   where the defendant creates a dangerous situation (e.g., *Miller* (1983));
(f)   where the defendant is under a duty to control others (e.g., *Tuck* v *Robinson* (1970) where a publican was convicted of aiding and abetting unlawful drinking due to his failure to prevent his customers from so doing).

An alternative way in which the above information might be expressed is to say:

Traditionally, English law has been reluctant to impose liability on people who have failed to act in a particular way, save in identifiable circumstances where they are deemed to be under a duty to act. First, . . .

Of course, it may be that over time the law has developed to the extent that the exceptions are so numerous as to 'eat up' the general rule and you may need a different (i.e., more appropriate) restatement of the relevant law. Alternatively, it may be that the area of law is confused and confusing and there is a great deal of difficulty in mapping out its exact parameters – for example, the law on recovery for pure economic loss. One way to deal with a difficult area like this is to focus on what is clear and *then* to move on to discuss the more debatable aspects of the issue.

Sometimes academics and/or judges are able to devise a rationale which explains the cases, and which can be used to good effect for exam purposes. Take, for example, the law on mistake in criminal law. Cases such as *Morgan* [1976] AC 182, HL, *Williams (Gladstone)* (1984) 78 Cr App R 276, CA, *Beckford* [1988] AC 130, PC, and *Kimber* (1984) 77 Cr App R 225, CA all support the proposition that the law will accept an honest, albeit unreasonable, mistake as to a definitional element of a crime (a subjective approach); whereas *Fotheringham* (1989) 88 Cr App R 207, CA, *O'Grady* [1987] QB 995, and *Graham* [1982] 1 WLR 294 would seem to support a more limited reading of the law on mistake – that perhaps in these circumstances only a reasonable mistake is relevant (an objective test). How can these two strands of case law be reconciled? One plausible explanation is that where the mistake relates to a justificatory defence (e.g., self-defence, consent etc.) the subjective view will suffice, but where the mistake relates to an excusatory defence (e.g., drunkenness, duress etc.) it must be reasonable.[1] This distinction is not something that

---

1.   See, Clarkson & Keating, *Criminal Law: Text and Materials* (3rd edn, Sweet & Maxwell, London, 1994), 263–4.

the judges sat down and decided before they gave judgments in the above cases. Instead, it is something which has been teased out of the decisions by someone who has sought to take an aerial view of the material in order to make (some) sense of it. On the basis of this justificatory/excusatory distinction, if a new case were to arise, we would have some idea of the way it would (and perhaps should) be decided and where it would (and perhaps should) fit into the legal framework. There is nothing fixed or rigid about the above classification – indeed in Anglo-American jurisprudence the distinction between justifications and excuses is ill-developed – but it does provide a framework with which to marshall the authorities. Note that cases which do not fit into an established classification are often described as anomalies.

B.   Answers where an argument is required

The key to writing a good essay answer is 'to pile up an argument, sentence by sentence to produce a powerful mixture of facts and opinions which wins the day'.[2] It would seem that most examiners 'favour bold, aggressive and "original" essay writing rather than [a] cautious, discursive [style]'.[3] Indeed, in the words of one examiner, an answer should have 'the punch of a *Sun* editorial and the persuasive concision of one of Alistair Cooke's "Letters from America"'.[4] But students' views – insofar as they offer views – tend to be less forthright. This is not surprising – it takes a lot of confidence to express an opinion about an issue which leading legal academics have discussed for years and to which they have failed to come up with a definitive solution – but while it may sometimes pay to be cautious, your examiner will sense if you are too deferential to the material under consideration and will mark you down accordingly. A common approach which students adopt is to put the question asked in context, recognising that there are arguments going both ways. They will then proceed to outline those arguments and in their conclusion (it is hoped) come down on one side or the other by doing one of two things either:

(a)   they will lurch off by saying 'In my opinion . . .', or 'I think . . . ' (by adopting this type of approach students give the impression that their views are tagged on at the end and are not a fully integrated part of the answer (which is entirely true)); or

(b)   they will say something like 'In the light of the above-mentioned criticisms, it seems that . . .' (and their view(s) follow on from this).

This whole approach is a very conventional way of tackling an essay question and, it must be said, if done properly, will score reasonable marks. But it is also a very pedestrian approach and tends to be unrewarding for an examiner to mark. It is, despite the begrudging decision to jump one way or the other, an

2.   *Independent on Sunday*, 22 May 1994.
3.   *Guardian*, 12 July 1994.
4.   Philip Thody, 'Top Marks for Restraint', *Times Higher Educational Supplement*, 15 July 1991.

exercise in fence-sitting – the favourite pastime of many exam candidates. The student is simply too tentative, too afraid to commit himself or herself to a particular point of view for fear of appearing biased or blinkered.

Although a partisan answer is a poor answer, it is better if you map out a point of view – posit a thesis – taking into account the fact that, while there are arguments going in the other direction, they can nonetheless be countered or minimised in view of other factors. In this way, you will have committed yourself to a particular position; you will have developed your own argument as to why you have done so; and your answer will be balanced in the sense that you will have recognised opposing arguments. Such an answer is difficult to construct, but is very rewarding to mark, and consequently, if done properly, will score very highly indeed.

The answer does not have to be original, or incredibly accomplished, but needs merely to be professional in the sense that it is both competently and confidently expressed. Examiners want to know what you think and why – indeed in the not too distant future someone may be paying you for your opinion. More generally, the examiner wants to know your argument: it is the *quality* of your written submission which the examiner marks, irrespective of whether you personally hold the argument that you present. Lawyers often argue points of view in court (quite convincingly) to which they are not necessarily committed.

Despite the fact that, as with problem answers, there is no one method with which to write a good essay answer, there are, nonetheless, recognised techniques which can be used to produce a polished answer. These are set out below and are illustrated by way of accompanying examples drawn from law journal articles, judgments, and student answers:

(a)   In addition to knowing where your essay is going to end up (i.e., which way you will jump), it is often a good idea to explain clearly the steps which you will take to get there. In other words, your answer is like a path that needs signposts to help the reader negotiate the material. For example, you should make clear different 'families' of arguments:

> There are four arguments which support this view. First, . . . Secondly, . . . Thirdly, . . . Lastly, . . . [Or **'The final argument that can be levelled against . . . is . . .':** **this reminds the reader which set of arguments you are discussing.**]

In a longer piece of work, e.g., a dissertation or a long essay, it may prove useful to break the material up with headings, and perhaps in your introduction briefly to outline what each section will discuss. A quick glance at many of the longer articles in any of the good law journals is illustrative of this point.

(b)   In helping to marshall your arguments, make good use of what might be called 'turning words' (i.e., words which indicate that the 'flow' of your argument is about to change direction). For example: however, but, yet, nevertheless, nonetheless, notwithstanding, despite this, by contrast. The same goes for 'reinforcing words', which are used to link up arguments which belong to the same 'family'. Examples include: likewise, similarly, moreover. Again, the use of such words should be clear from a quick glance at any well-written piece.

(c)   It may be helpful at times to employ what are often called 'strawmen' arguments (i.e., arguments which go against your thesis, but which you specifically caricature so that you can shoot them down). Remember, however, that *your* argument will be weakened if you misrepresent an argument which goes against the case you are trying to make. It is probably best to do justice to competing arguments and then to go on to show how they are fallacious or unsatisfactory in some significant respect. For example, Lord Templeman, from his judgment in the controversial House of Lords decision in *Brown* [1993] 2 WLR 554 says:

> [A] [I]t was said, every person has a right to deal with his body as he pleases. [B] I do not consider that this slogan provides a sufficient guide to the policy decision which must now be made. [C] It is an offence for a person to abuse his body by taking drugs. Although the law is often broken, the criminal law restrains a practice which is regarded as dangerous and injurious to individuals and which if allowed and extended is harmful to society generally. [D] In any event, the appellants in this case did not mutilate their own bodies. They inflicted bodily harm on willing victims. [C] Suicide is no longer an offence but a person who assists another to commit suicide is guilty of murder or manslaughter.

[A]   Lord Templeman outlines a proposition (with which he does not agree).
[B]   He criticises the proposition for being too wide.
[C]   He then provides an example.
[D]   He attempts to strengthen his argument, by distinguishing the initial proposition from the case before him.

Although few would say that the speeches in *Brown* represent models of coherent reasoning, the above does indicate the sort of techniques that can be employed.

(d)   Outline the general principle or abstract position first and then follow up with a concrete example. The extract in (c) above is illustrative of this point:

> [I]t was said, every person has a right to deal with his body as he pleases. I do not consider that this slogan provides a sufficient guide to the policy decision which must now be made. It is an offence for a person to abuse his body by taking drugs.

(e)   Arguments can be expressed in the negative. For example:

> Just because the UK lacks a Bill of Rights, it does not mean that rights play no part in our legal system.

(f)   Your answer should demonstrate your ability to make fine distinctions. For example, you may agree with the outcome of a decision, but deplore the reasoning used to justify it (because although the outcome may be 'just' on the facts of the case, the reasoning may be too broad and thus lead to an unwarranted extension of the rule outlined). A classic example is *Caldwell* [1982] AC 341 – almost everyone would agree with the outcome but many have claimed that the decision is too wide (it fails to take into account whether the defendant has the *capacity* to appreciate the risk).

(g)   As with cases, do not be led by the academic authorities. Rather, impose your own structure on the material you have been asked to consider. You need to use the academic authorities – much as you use cases – as examples of different ways of viewing the problem. In other words, avoid a long list of different views which academics hold: 'Atiyah thinks that . . . **Treital** believes . . . Collins argues . . . [and so on]'.

(h)   Familiarise yourself with appropriate 'lawyerly' language. For example: 'this interpretation would emasculate the Act'; 'there exists a lacuna in the legislation'; 'a question arises whether the common law is abrogated'; 'this is yet another decision which signals a judicial retreat from . . . '; 'there is some support for this proposition from the case law'; 'this line of reasoning was seized on in a more recent decision'; and so on. By the same token, avoid incomplete expressions like 'A will be liable'. Liable for what?

(i)   One last point. Some law examiners prefer you to express your views in terms of impartial submissions (e.g., 'therefore it is submitted that . . .') rather than 'I think . . .'. Other examiners, however, prefer you to be more direct (honest?); your answer is, after all, personal and subjective, and to try to cover it with a veil of false objectivity is disingenuous. Nonetheless, nearly all examiners will be appalled by 'In my opinion', 'I feel that . . .', or worse, 'I personally think . . .'. Instead, try 'In this essay I will argue that . . .', or, in summing up, 'I have argued that . . .' or 'My argument is . . .'. Whatever approach you adopt, do not let it become instrusive.

To summarise, to turn out a good answer you need to make effective use of these techniques. Your models in this respect should be the books, articles, casenotes, and judgments you are asked to read. Simon Gardner's, 'Duress in Attempted Murder' (1991) 107 LQR 389, provides a good example of some of the points discussed above:

> The Court of Appeal has decided that duress is no defence to attempted murder: *R* v *Gotts* [1991] 2 WLR 878. In *R* v *Howe* [1987] AC 417 the House of Lords had decided that duress was no defence to murder itself, [hence] the extension of this rule to the attempt might have been thought predictable. However, an examination of the decision raises questions about its sustainability – and, in turn, that of *Howe* . . .

There, in the space of a few lines, Gardner summarises the law and, more importantly for the purposes of illustration here, sets out his stall: telling us exactly what he hopes the note will achieve. The rest of the note justifies this point of view.

He also demonstrates other points. For example:

> **[A]** Late in 1990, terrorists persuaded members of the public, by holding hostage their families, to drive vehicles loaded with explosives into military checkpoints . . .. According to *Howe* these drivers were guilty of murder. It appears that, on the contrary, they are not being charged with any offence. The practical disposal of the case again reveals dissatisfaction with the principle of *Howe*. **[B]** It might be rejoined here . . . that *Howe* should be read as allowing for the non-prosecution of meritorious cases of murder under duress . . . their Lordships in *Howe* took this very point . . . . **[C]** But . . . only the clutched straw of unreviewable executive discretion prevents this from being a flat contradiction of the fundamental proposition [outlined in *Howe*] that for moral or instrumental reasons murder under duress cannot be pardoned.

[A]   Gardner criticises of the rationale in *Howe*.

[B]   He then sets up a counter argument.

[C]   He hits this counter argument 'for six', reinforcing his favoured position.

We are left in no doubt as to where Gardner stands: he likes neither the decision in *Howe* nor the reasons used to support it. His short note has all the hallmarks of the sort of approach which you should try to emulate.

Consider also the following passage from Lord Oliver in *Murphy* v *Brentwood* [1991] AC 398:

> It does not, of course, follow as a matter of necessity from the mere fact that the only damage suffered by a plaintiff in an action for the tort of negligence is pecuniary . . . that his claim is bound to fail. **[This is Lord Oliver's broad statement of principle, expressed in the negative.]** It is true, in an uninterrupted line of cases since 1875, it has been consistently held that a third party cannot successfully sue in tort for the interference with his economic expectations . . . resulting from injury to the person or property of another person with whom he has or is likely to have a contractual relationship **[recognising a potential line of argument which could go against his initial proposition; note that he actually bolsters this line of argument with a list of authorities not quoted here]** . . . But, it is far from clear from these decisions that the reason for the plaintiffs' failure was simply that the only loss sustained was 'economic' **[questioning the ambit of the authorities he has cited]**. Rather, they seem to have been based either upon the remoteness of the damage as a matter of direct causation or, more probably, upon the 'floodgates' argument of the impossibility of containing liability within any acceptable bounds if the law were to permit such claims to proceed **[providing the basis for limiting the authorities; in a passage which comes directly afterwards, Lord Oliver goes on to support his argument with a number of cases]**.

Here you can trace a 'flow' to the passage. Lord Oliver advances his argument by way of recognising an alternative means of looking at the issue, the extent of which he is able to circumscribe.

Consider also, the 'flow' of the following example:

[A] Proposition X has much to commend it. First, . . . Secondly, . . . Thirdly, . . . Lastly, . . . **[B]** However, serious weaknesses have been identified. For example, . . . **[C]** Nonetheless, . . . **[D]** On balance, therefore, it would seem preferable that X . . . **[Or 'Notwithstanding the difficulties . . .']**.

[A] Main argument.
[B] Criticism of main argument.
[C] Criticism of criticism.
[D] Conclusion which again supports main argument.

Alternatively, you could structure it as follows:

On first impressions proposition X has little to commend it. First, . . . Secondly, . . . Thirdly, . . . Lastly, . . . **[B]** However, on closer inspection these arguments are seriously flawed because . . . **[C]** It would seem therefore that X is preferable.

Here you are recognising that there are weaknesses in your favoured approach, but you are demonstrating that these so-called 'weaknesses' are themselves open to criticism (misconceived, irrelevant, and so on). Try to end with your most forceful arguments. Remember that much of what you are doing relates to the art of persuasion.

The rest of this chapter is devoted to applying some of the above-mentioned techniques to a specific exam question on the criminal law of omissions. In particular, we aim to set out the relevant arguments for and against certain propositions and to demonstrate how this 'raw' material can be fashioned to write answers with contrasting conclusions.

Question

English criminal law should either introduce a general duty to act to save imperilled persons, or, alternatively, expand the present list of situations when one is under a duty to act.

Discuss.

One of the suggestions which has been made in this area is the introduction of a duty of 'easy rescue' (Ashworth, 'The Scope of Criminal Liability for Omissions' (1989) 105 LQR 424).

There are sound arguments in favour of a duty of easy rescue:

(a)   it is immoral not to render assistance when it is well within one's powers to do so; criminal law should be a reflection of a moral world;

(b)   attention should be focused on punishing conduct which causes a particular harm irrespective of whether the harm results from an act of commission or omission;

(c)   arguments that a general duty to act would be contrary to individual liberty and autonomy ignore the value that individuals place on interpersonal support and relationships;

(d)   the law is justified in using coercion to force people to take actions required to improve the options and opportunities of others;

(e)   the reduction in the autonomy of an individual will be offset as the level of autonomy in the community as a whole rises.

At the same time there are a number of forceful objections, both in principle and in practice, to this line of argument:

(a)   *Objections in principle*:

(i)   criminal liability is premised on our concepts of *mens rea* and *actus reus*, which denote control – these are relevant to positive actions rather than a failure to counter a risk not caused by the defendant;

(ii)   it will inhibit people's personal autonomy;

(iii)   the difficulty of establishing the requisite causal link between the defendant's inactivity and the harms that occur (a person cannot 'cause' a result by doing nothing);

(iv)   values such as charity or courage will be eroded because people will have no real choice but to act in accordance with the law;

(v)   there is something morally repugnant about holding an individual responsible for an independent process over which he or she exerts no control;

(vi)   'luck' would be allowed to play an unwarranted part in the criminal law, e.g., the unlucky bystander who is under an obligation to rescue;

(vii)   the wealthy person who fails to give to the starving beggar would be liable for a criminal offence – such a law could undermine the capitalist work ethic;

(viii) since a general duty can be defined only in broad terms, prosecutors would have too much discretion – this breaches the principle of maximum certainty (liability should be well defined).

(b)   *Pragmatic objections*:

(i)   the jury in the safety of court might have a different view of what is 'easy rescue';

(ii)   an incompetent rescuer could cause more harm than good;

(iii)   who would be the rescuer in a crowd of people.

Answer A

In 'The Scope of Criminal Liability for Omissions', Ashworth argues for a duty of 'easy rescue' where no unreasonable risk, cost, or inconvenience would be incurred by the potential rescuer. Yet despite its superficial attractions, fundamental problems are caused by the expansion in criminal liability that a new general duty of easy rescue would entail. In any case the existing categories of criminal liability are adequate.

The case for a general duty to act to save imperilled persons rests on the view that it is clearly immoral not to render assistance when it is well within one's powers to do so. The criminal law should be a reflection of a moral world; attention should be focused on punishing conduct which causes a particular harm irrespective of whether the harm is a result of commission or omission. Arguments that such a general duty to act would be contrary to individual liberty and autonomy ignore the value that individuals place on interpersonal support and relationships. As Raz argues, the law is justified in using coercion to force people to take actions required to improve the options and opportunities of others. The reduction in the autonomy of an individual will be offset as the level of autonomy in the community as a whole rises.

While forceful, these arguments are by no means compelling. As Meade argues, forcing the individual to give attention to others in itself represents a threat to his own autonomy. If society is prepared to sacrifice an individual's autonomy in order to save a life, how many other rights of individuals will be ignored for some – supposedly justifiable – greater good? Furthermore, forcing people to act through fear of legal sanction would involve the erosion of important values such as courage or charity . . .

* * *

[You could then discuss the adequacy of existing categories of liability; see above at pp. 113.]

Answer B

This question asks us to consider alternative ways of improving the criminal law of omissions. In order to answer this it is first necessary to explain why the existing law is inadequate. I will then go on to consider the suitability of the different reform options which have been mooted.

Weaknesses in the existing law
[Here you could discuss the weaknesses in the current law, e.g., a bystander who watches a small child die when rescue was easy is not liable.]

Moral justification for extension
[Here you could outline the arguments to support an extension of the existing duty.]

Limitations of duty
[Here you could outline arguments to limit this duty based on practical problems; your ultimate argument could be that the defendant should not be liable for the 'full' offence, but for a specific offence of 'failure to act'.]

Conclusion
[Here you could say that a 'failure to act' approach satisfies the moral need to punish, while at the same time recognising fundamental philosophical and practical objections to holding people liable for the full offence.]

As you can see, the same material has been used to produce contrasting answers, potentially of equal worth. Answer A presents an argument in favour of the status quo, while Answer B suggests that reform is needed and indicates how it may be satisfactorily achieved. Whatever the desirability of one conclusion over the other, both answers reflect a fair degree of sophistication and clarity and, prima facie, merit the award of high marks.

Conclusion

The array of techniques we have identified that students must use to perform successfully in exams may seem daunting. However, the advice we offer should not be allowed to obscure our central point, namely, that aside from having a good knowledge of the material, the most important aspect of any written task is structure. The material must be presented in some form of digestible package. This is something with which judges (in writing their judgments), barristers (in writing opinions), academics (in writing articles and books), and students (in writing exams) must all struggle. As examiners – and indeed as former students – we have tried to lay down some of the ground rules. The ball is now in *your* court.